JOURNEY TO NOWHERE

JOURNEY TO NOWHERE

THE SAGA OF THE NEW UNDERCLASS

by
DALE MAHARIDGE

photographs by
MICHAEL WILLIAMSON

THE DIAL PRESS
DOUBLEDAY & COMPANY, INC.
GARDEN CITY, NEW YORK
1985

Book design by Beverley Vawter Gallegos

Library of Congress Cataloging in Publication Data
Maharidge, Dale.
Journey to nowhere.
1. Unemployed—United States.   2. United States—
Economic conditions—1981–   . 3. United States—
Social conditions—1980–   . I. Title.
HD5724.M232 1984   305′.90694   83-45195
ISBN 0-385-27964-7
ISBN 0-385-27965-5 (pbk.)

DEDICATION

From Williamson: To Brenda, who stayed with this hobo for richer and poorer; to all the Farm Security Administration photographers who documented the last depression so well; and to Dick Schmidt, mentor and friend.

From Maharidge: To Diane Alters, Elizabeth Fernandez, Judith Haynes, Jenni Laidman, Catherine Warren, and Miss Barton, my tenth-grade teacher who insisted I someday write a book. All have helped.

From both of us: To those whom you will read about in these pages.

ACKNOWLEDGMENTS

We extend deep appreciation to Bill Moore, a city editor who, in his brief reign at the Sacramento *Bee*, rose above the mediocrity that plagues most newspapers and gave us the idea that made this book possible; and to James W. Fitzgerald, Jr., and Allen H. Peacock, our editors at Doubleday who recognized the importance of this project and shepherded us on our way.

Thanks also go out to John and Susan Russo, who allowed us to live in their Youngstown home and forgave us for breaking their weird coffeepot; Julius Simchick, who provided the history of steel in the Mahoning Valley; and Carlos Rosales, an El Paso *Times* photographer who showed us around Juárez, Mexico.

CONTENTS

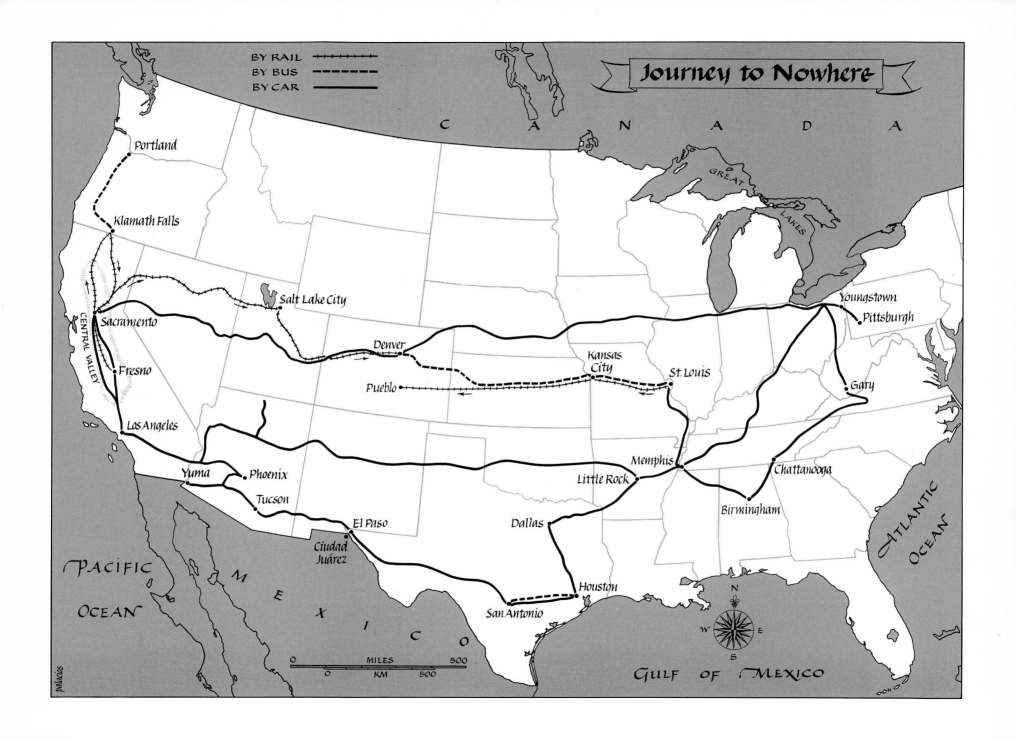

INTRODUCTION

They are young, old, smart, dumb, good, bad, your neighbor, your brother, businessmen, steelworkers, hotel owners—anybody. They crossed the threshold. They lost their jobs, can't find jobs, or are underemployed, working a few hours a week at the federal minimum. They were cut off, like a gangrenous finger, from unemployment benefits. They are too proud for welfare, or cannot get it. They have hit bottom.

Forget the aimless Beat Generation of the 1950s. The brief moment of the We Generation of the 1960s. The Me Generation of the 1970s. The next decade or more seems to be the time of the Out Generation. It's the era of the disenfranchised worker, left out of jobs, left out of the system, forgotten.

Members of the Out Generation are not just victims of the latest recession. The rippling of the economy between recessions, recoveries, and the threat of more recessions doesn't mean much to a lot of these folks. Recoveries mean it is getting better—if you've already got it made. Fundamental changes are disrupting the labor market. Much of the shifting job picture is occurring in American industry, which is in decay. Industries continue to move out of this country, shut down, automate, or demand wage cuts, killing jobs, transforming thousands of workers into pariahs of the new "technocaste" system, a two-class society. The winners are those able to cope with deindustrialization.

The Out Generation, the losers—those too old or unable to be retrained for fields like high tech, too young to already have a piece of the action, or simply the odd men out in the game of musical chairs for a shrinking number of jobs—seem doomed to unemployment or low-paying jobs for a long time to come.

Some of the people on the downside of this change hit the road in search of work, or because they have nowhere else to turn. They are the new class of hobo and street person.

For the most part, they are a strong breed, survivors, unchristened heroes. They are on a voyage . . . into the darkened alleys of their minds . . . down the endless highways and lonely rail lines of America.

This book is the story of a few of those journeys.

Some names have been changed for those who, out of embarrassment, asked for anonymity, and for those who would be particularly sensitive or ashamed. They need *not be ashamed, of course, but try telling that to someone just thrust into the new underclass. In other instances, real identities are used.*

I will tell you a bit about us and how we got involved in this adventure. We were simply chroniclers who tried to remain invisible as we journeyed with these men and women across the nation—unshaven, wearing bandannas on our heads, packs on our backs, and toting a tiny notebook and a camera or two.

It was a slow news day. The kind of day that made me wonder why I became a reporter—an often dull, plodding profession. Adventure and stories of unknown worlds pleading to be written were waiting somewhere. I was thinking I'd rather be Out There—Alaska, the Amazon, a cornfield in Nebraska. Anywhere.

But not here, in the Sacramento *Bee* newsroom.

I had resigned myself to spending an eternity staring at a sickly green computer screen when I was approached by Bill Moore, then my city editor, who had just come from some sleazy downtown bar. He'd met an aged hobo there who told him jobless middle-class people are riding the rails, just like in the Great Depression. Go Out There, said Moore (a hobo of sorts himself), ride the trains, and learn what's going on.

The next day, I found myself standing at the edge of a railroad yard. My heart galloped. I had never been in a train yard before. Tar and oil stuck to my feet as I tiptoed from tie to tie between the tracks. Rippling heat punched my face.

I approached some scruffy old hoboes. Nervously, I offered cigarettes. I don't smoke, but learned to Out There. (It would become part of the disguise. I quickly learned that cigarettes are a passport to meeting people in the street world.) They were glad to talk to someone who was actually going to listen. Hell, they said, there are too many new-timers out here . . . since the economy went to hell, they're cramming the missions . . . you can't even find a boxcar empty of the damn greenhorns.

I realized at once that there would have to be pictures. The pain and despair in the faces I saw told the story as well as words did. I ran back to the office and recruited Williamson.

Within days—at 2 A.M., April 25, 1982, to be precise—we hopped a northbound out of Sacramento. For one week we rode the rails up and down the length of California. We found many of the people we were looking for, people who had worked hard all their lives but now could not beg a job. It hit us hard. We saw something, but weren't sure what.

Their eyes haunted us. They told us they'd been places, seen things.

We desperately wanted to see through those eyes, to understand. But we'd only visited their world. Something big was happening to America, and we'd only caught a glimpse.

In the coming months, we immersed ourselves in the world of the unemployed. And still we did not see. There was something more, something we were missing.

Then that world came closer. An aunt of mine too young for retirement and too old to be reemployed was laid off from her job in Cleveland. A grade-school buddy with an engineering degree was on the streets of Portland, Oregon. Williamson's friend was losing his mind because he couldn't find work.

It was time for us to plunge into the world of the unemployed, if we were to see. But how?

We noticed the unemployed came from every part of the country, but the tentacles of the problem seemed to emanate from the industrial heartland. To understand the future of

America, and what causes formerly middle-class people to wind up living on the street, we would have to understand the decline of the industrial core of the nation.

We elected to travel about the country for three months by car, by rail, by foot, by thumb, beginning in Youngstown, Ohio. We chose it as a starting point because it typifies the agony of dozens of Midwestern cities. Beyond Youngstown, we had no specific plans other than to head aimlessly west, as do many of the jobless.

I was born in the industrial heartland, near Cleveland, not far from Youngstown. My father worked as a grinder for one of the biggest machine tool companies in the world. An uncle worked on an automobile assembly line. My grandfather once worked in a steel mill, in front of an open-hearth furnace in the Flats of Cleveland. When I graduated from high school, I too, for a time, worked in factories. I didn't know what to expect of my homeland after an absence of several years.

Just hours after our plane landed in Cleveland, we picked a $600 car out of a newspaper ad and went to look at it. It was a big old Detroit monster ("a real tuna boat," said Williamson), the body rat-bitten with rust, tires bald as an armadillo's backside, but with a tight front end, good brakes, and a sweet-sounding engine.

We bought the car and were soon careening through a snowstorm toward Youngstown, skidding through the night down ice-slick streets, wondering what was Out There. Wondering if we would see.

This is the kind of work that was once done in the Youngstown mills. This man, a scarfer, torches the steel after it is rolled to remove blemishes.
It is one of the toughest jobs in a mill.

Chapter 1: HOW IT WAS

Steel country . . . Youngstown, Ohio . . . early . . . a morning typical of thousands of others, of a time not so long ago.

Daylight breaks over the low-slung rim of the Mahoning Valley. Steel mills materialize amid the vanishing darkness, looming strong and powerful, assaulting the senses with a wonderful confusion of rust, dust, coke, and smoke. Flames leap against the orange sky, celebrating the tawdry poetry of clanging metal and sizzling blast furnaces, the meaty, macho odor of roasting iron ore that tastes thick and good on the tongue.

These deities of the industrial revolution are big beyond comprehension. Each mill is more than one mile long and half as wide, commanding the center of attention in a head-to-toe parade for miles down the narrow valley.

Planted on the hillsides are neat white clapboard row houses, meekly overlooking the bullies that belch an avalanche of soot each day. The grime stains the dwellings and cars parked in the narrow drives, but isn't minded. The mills paid for the homes and cars, and they're allowed to dirty them.

Steel is sovereign here, and steel will never let the men forget it. Inside those homes they stir, waking to the grumble of gears echoing across the valley, churning from deep within the bellies of the mills; the same lonely tune that lulled them to sleep. It's time for the new shift—the changing of the guard. A tide of humanity begins moving. Workers rush from their homes, still buckling their trousers. They pass men coming from the mills, who wipe a night's worth of sweat and cinder dirt from their faces.

Incoming workers—blast furnace operators, scarfers, boilermakers—scatter to all parts of the mill. Those employed in the blooming mill, where the steel is rolled into usable sheets, are greeted by an inferno called the soaking pit, a flaming cavern where an angry supernova is held captive. They shield their faces from the blazing heat that reflects off their hardhats and goggles with an igneous glow.

The sleepy-eyed men are staring into hell. And hell is beautiful.

Hell is full of refrigerator-sized chunks of fresh, near-molten steel being grabbed up by a claw dropped from a city-block-long bridge crane three stories overhead. With the precision of a crab nipping at a bit of food, the talon swings one cube of steel at a time to a conveyor belt. The cubes are whisked away into the smoking abyss to be scrunched and beaten in a shower of sparks by a set of mandibles and rollers that heave like thunderclaps. In the end, at the other side of the blooming mill one-half mile away, the steel begins whirring through the rollers at a speed of sixty miles an hour, transformed into a sheet four feet wide and over one mile long, destined to be made into cars and washing machines.

The only light invading these chambers are thin rays of sun that sneak through scattered cracks in the ancient walls. Like laser beams, they spotlight sections of the machine—crusted with a century-old mascara of grease and rust—with a holy funereal glow.

Nothing is small in a steel mill. Man is reduced in scale to an ant crawling across a V-8 engine.

The machine dominates. But steelmaking is more than machines. It is these workers who make the metal live, thousands in each mill. And the steel is alive, the men passionately insist. Look . . . listen . . . smell! It gleams! It hisses! It sighs!

To these men, steel is more than a blend of coke, ore and limestone. There is another ingredient: their souls. "Smoke and blood is the mix of steel," poet Carl Sandburg wrote of the men of Youngstown in 1920.

The men are proud of their work. We are the best damn steelmakers in the world, you hear them brag in bars with names like the Open Hearth, the Flat Iron Cafe, or the Worker's Tavern.

If the men worship steel and the machines, it's easy to understand why. Steel has been good to Youngstown. Their grandfathers and fathers worked in the mills. And their sons are destined to follow. The American Dream is wrought in steel for the city of Youngstown. The history of steel in the Mahoning Valley is the history of America.

It began in 1803, when James and Daniel Heaton discovered iron ore lining the banks of Yellow Creek just south of Youngstown. A blast furnace was hastily built, and it was followed by others in the next years that provided the stoves, plows, and pans used by pioneers as they moved west and settled the nation.

Mahoning Valley iron helped win its first military conflict when the factories went into cannonball production during the Civil War. So important were the mills that they were the target of a commando raid by Confederate forces. The raid was not successful.

With the coming of the main thrust of the industrial revolution around the turn of the century, the demand for steel exploded. Steel was needed for bridges, buildings, ships and then cars as America expanded at home and abroad. The industrialists chose Youngstown as a major site for their big mills and Bessemer converters that had replaced the smaller stone blast furnaces.

Youngstown steel traveled the world. Youngstown steel was used in the gates of the newly opened Panama Canal. Youngstown steel helped win World War I and World War II, when the mills worked around the clock to produce metal for tanks and bombs. (The mills also fashioned steel for less popular wars in Korea and Vietnam.) When the second great war ended, Youngstown steel helped build the prosperity that followed. At one time, twenty-eight blast furnaces churned out molten iron, and more steel was made in Youngstown than in any other city in the nation.

Youngstown epitomized all that was good about the industrial revolution. It proudly called itself Steel Valley, the American equivalent of Europe's Ruhr Valley. Anyone could come to Youngstown and make it. The mills begged for workers, a slave class to labor seven days a week, twelve hours a day, for meager wages, until they rebelled in the riots of 1916, burned much of East Youngstown to the ground, and got a union. Steel continued to thrive and now so did the workers. The money lured thousands of immi-

Working steel mill on the Ohio River, Mingo Junction, Ohio. A truck hauls rolled steel to a distant market.

Working mill, Mingo Junction, Ohio.

grants from Old World countries—Poles, Slovaks, Italians, Hungarians—who flooded the city following World War I. Homes sprung up on the hillsides surrounding the mills. It became a fine city with a metropolitan population of one-half million served by a symphony, parks, museums, and libraries.

Word of the good life in Youngstown reached the Marshall family in the village of Ruzomberok, Czechloslovakia. It was during the height of the Great Depression when Martin Marshall brought his thirteen-year-old son Joe and the rest of his family to Youngstown. The young "Hunkie," as Joe was derisively called by those who had lived there longer, began working in a bakery.

Two years later, when Joe's father had a stroke and could no longer work, Joe had to get a real job that paid real money so he could support his family. His mother marched him down to the employment office on Market Street and lied that her boy was eighteen. The next day, Joe found himself working at Republic Steel.

Being young, small, and a Hunkie, Joe was given the worst job in the mill. He became a riveter's helper. His job was to crawl under the ore cars and hold rivets in place with a metal pole while a worker above drove them. But the space was narrow—he couldn't fit both his head and hands in the crack to hold the pole and at the same time see what he was doing. So he had to support the steel rod with his forehead, while the other worker drove the rivet with 150 pounds of air pressure.

Hot sparks would shower his face and burn him. It was not an easy job. But it fed his family.

In 1942 Joe got a better job at U.S. Steel's Ohio Works. The mill was soon working at capacity for the war effort. Uncle Sam would call the tough young steelworker in 1944. Joe was wounded when he landed on Utah Beach in Normandy. Out of his battalion of 867, he was one of only four survivors.

Joe returned home to his job at the Ohio Works. He became a stationary engineer, tending the steam engines that pump air into the blast furnaces. He married, had a son and daughter, and lived in his father's home across from Calvary Cemetery. When his son graduated from high school, he too became a stationary engineer and joined his father in the mill.

They were part of the seemingly endless cycle of son following Dad into the mills. The mills provided security, and families were close. Few people ever moved more than a few miles from where they were born. Life was good for the Marshalls, and the city of Youngstown.

Homes planted on hillsides overlook the mills.

The shell of the Brier Hill Works.

Chapter 2: **THE RUST BOWL**

Joe Marshall surveys the barren, lifeless landscape unfolding before him, a mile-long Pompeii of rubble and rust, his jaws clamped as tight and expressionless as a garden toad's mouth.

He looks south. An empty sky greets him, a sky once filled with smoke billowing from the ten-story blast furnaces at Youngstown Sheet and Tube's Campbell Works. The turbines are mute. No longer do ore trains scurry back and forth. They remain forever sided on the tracks. Silent. Dead. Rusting under the burden of late winter snows.

His eyes follow a hawk winging its way north, soaring over the cold Brier Hill Works. In front of him is the Ohio Works. This mill is not just deceased like the other two, but has been dynamited and leveled.

He takes it all in, then his mouth creeps open. A painful sigh oozes out. Joe places his arm around his son. Together, they venture into the ruins where they and thirty-five hundred others once worked.

The plant site is within walking distance of their home, but until today neither man has visited here in the three years since that painful day still etched in their minds: April 6, 1980. The day the world changed. The day their part of the mill closed.

A lot of other Youngstowners have seen their world change since the first of the mills shut down—the Campbell Works—on Black Monday, September 19, 1977. In the next few years, the great mills fell like broken promises.

The golden era of industrialism—and Youngstown—is over. And over sixty thousand people in the tiny Mahoning Valley are out of work because of it.

The father and son walk on. The younger Marshall opens his wallet empty of money and produces his union card. Yes, he says, pointing to the date on the card, it was ten years ago today that he was hired at this mill. It reminds him of the days when his pocket was full of cash and he would have celebrated the anniversary.

"This is incredible," Joe Jr. mutters. He stoops and clutches a piece of coke with his large hand, a hand that has enjoyed hard work, joined to an arm as tough as pig iron. He fondles the charred lump of coal and keeps repeating the word "incredible," as if saying it over and over will change things. "I don't want to look at this place."

But they continue down a pathway that led into the plant—a sidewalk that now leads nowhere, flanked by a chaos of heaped bricks and blocks of concrete studded with twisted reinforcing rods that reach out like ferrous snakes.

Joe Marshall and Joe Marshall, Jr., walk through the ruins of the mill where they used to work.

The dynamited Ohio Works.

"For thirty-seven and a half years, I walked this sidewalk," white-haired Joe Sr. says in a voice as gravelly as the steam engine he once tended. "Back there were the open hearths. Over there, six blast furnaces. They'd just rebuilt numbers three and five. Over there, a ten-million-gallon pump. There's where the Bessemer blow room was. I worked there most of my life. This was a good place to work. A good place to live. We weren't obsolete! We were the best!"

They point. They look. They remember.

One wall remains standing. Scrawled on it in faded blue paint are the words "I jus wanna celebrate another day of working."

"Our plants will never reopen," says Joe Jr. "They're tearing them down. Of all my friends, only two are working."

The older man casts a vexed look at his son. "In the Depression, they closed factories. Now, they're blowing them up! I'm worried about Joe. I've got to help Joe. Us, the older people, we're going to die out. But what about Joe?"

Joe Jr. frowns. He sighs, "Oh, Dad," with a barely perceptible nasal accent. But his father's concerns are valid. The past three years haven't been kind to young Joe. He's traveled all over Ohio and even to California looking for work. Daily, he fills out applications. He's forgotten how many times he's stood in line with hundreds of other men for a chance at a job. It's hard to find employment when you're twenty-nine and have been trained to operate a machine that was obsolete in 1910.

Finally, he had to move back home. His $19,000 savings account has been reduced to a few hundred bucks. "The only thing keeping me here is that I don't have the money to drive around and look for work anymore. Without my parents," he says, "I'd probably be dead."

Now, Joe studies law enforcement at the university. He hopes to make it his new career. So far, all it's gotten him is a job as an undercover armed security guard for a few hours a week at a local grocery chain. Youngstown grocery stores never used to have armed guards. Now, the men with money fear the thousands who are penniless, and their worry has created some work for Joe.

Joe says he will not shoot anyone for stealing food. He'll let them take it.

"This is a miserable way to live," says young Joe. "I don't want to live with my parents. When my parents were my age, they had a house and a kid."

Does he want that?

Hell, yeah!" he says sharply, leaning forward on a mound of bricks that he punches with his fist, his muscular frame outlined by the jagged Brier Hill Works. "I *want* that."

Joe's father has had enough of memories. He walks back to the car, passing beneath a sign that reads U.S. Steel— We're Involved. He shakes his head.

"How could they shut it down? It was so big. You could hear the noise from this place at my house." The older man pauses. "It's quiet now."

The wind punctuates his words.

"What Hitler couldn't do, they did it for him."

Back at the weed-choked parking lot, Joe Jr. points to the empty but still-standing office building of U.S. Steel, to the door of the employment office where he was hired. He then motions to the entrance next to it, the door he and five hundred others hammered down in a fit of rage when they stormed the executive offices after the closing was announced. Joe had a lot of anger back then. Now, there's nothing left to get mad at.

"For a town our size, look what we put out. No one could match Youngstown. We helped build America. What they did was rape Youngstown," says young Joe, slamming the car door. "This was our work car. Now, we use it for the dog."

The sedan speeds up Steel Street.

That night at home, the Marshall family watches tele-

The Marshall family at home, Joe Sr., Joe and Kay, Joe's mother.

vision while their dog, Duke, lounges on the living-room floor. They see commercials that are part of a million-dollar advertising campaign by the Republican Party, telling them President Ronald Reagan's economic policies are working. The recession is over. America is back to work.

The dead steel mills stand as pathetic mausoleums to the decline of American industrial might that was once the envy of the world.

The decaying hulks are a constant reminder to Youngstowners of the good days. Now, they look strangely out of place, misplaced medieval cities of rusting iron.

We enter the Brier Hill Works. We pause at the beginning of a long twilit corridor that leads to the interior of the ghost factory. It is a place inhabited by spirits. They do not want us to enter. We walk on, with caution.

Our feet striking metal floors create echoes of hollow laughter. We drop into the ore pits, subterranean dungeons full of rushing water that once held a million tons of taconite ore, coke, and limestone. Secret passages with icicles like daggers hanging from the ceiling lead off into darkness. Mounds of taconite still fill the pits, waiting expectantly to be made into iron.

We hurry from that black hole to Jeanette, the blast furnace that once produced seven hundred tons of metal a day. The floor around its base is littered with tools dropped on the last day of work six years earlier. Iron ladles are scattered about, resembling twelve-foot-long sugar spoons. Over there, a pair of goggles. Here, a pair of shoes. Slag, frozen where it cooled, drips like tears at the base of the furnace.

Time is suspended. It seems workers could reappear at any moment and start making iron. But this can never happen. A blast furnace runs twenty-four hours a day and must never shut down. When it does, it cools, causing the cracking of interior fire brick that contains the magma of molten iron. It would cost many hundreds of thousands of dollars to rebuild. Not to mention the millions it would take to refurbish the rest of the plant.

Once the heat is gone from a steel mill, it is like a dead body. Nothing short of divine intervention can bring it back.

"I guess we're down," says Ken Platt, seated at the kitchen table of his home. It is midday, a time he'd normally be working. His mouth puckers and wrinkles and he exhales somberly, resting his red-bearded head on the pillar of his arm. The fingers of his free hand nervously tap the formica. The giant smokestack of a man—father of 5- and 8-year-old kids—has only worked a few weeks in the past year at his job as a millwright at Republic Steel's rolling mill.

"This is the worst off I've been since I was fifteen. I've always worked. We worked seven days a week. We just about lived there. Now, we're nobody. We don't matter. My wife's brother was a good worker. Now, he questions his self-worth. He drinks. I don't think he could work anymore. It's like something rotting away."

He hates the thought of America's waning industrial might. His fist comes alive and slams the table with such force it makes us leap backward.

"We're supposed to be the best country in the world! Why can't we have better? We're going to wind up like England. The companies want to pay less wages. When you make minimum wage, you invest in bread and bologna. How can the economy survive like that? I can't afford a new car. I'm scared to spend $100. I used to say people on welfare were cheating. Now, I know better.

"The mill is run by a steam engine built in 1908. It's very crude. When something breaks, we make the part. They never buy anything. When you walk in there, you step back to 1915. I blame the companies. They should have a responsibility to the community. They should have re-invested."

Inside a dead mill.

The view from the top
of the ten-story Brier Hill
blast furnace.

Blow Room, the Brier Hill Works.

Locker room, Brier Hill Works.

Locker room.

I ask David Roderick, chairman of U.S. Steel—the biggest steel company in America—why his firm, in part, helped kill Youngstown by closing the Ohio Works.

And the chairman replies the mill had become antiquated and steel markets had changed. The workers were given severance and pension benefits, and he feels that ends U.S. Steel's responsibility to Youngstown. "I don't think the corporation can in perpetuity become the saviour of a community."

Yes, management was partly at fault for not buying new machinery to keep U.S. Steel mills competitive . . . but so were the workers for demanding so much in wages, the chairman insists. Big steel is trying to save itself, he says.

"I'm on the side of the angels here."

Who or what killed the mills?

The workers blame the industrialists; the industrialists blame the workers. Both groups blame foreign steel imports brought into this country at below cost; severe recession, the worst since the Great Depression; environmental regulations.

Much larger forces are at work, however.

A changing world is responsible, a world in which not only steel but other heavy industries have been dethroned. America is entering an age of uncertainty, said to be ruled by computers and high technology. Youngstown is just one city among many dozens that has become the victim of deindustrialization.

America will always make steel, cars, and other industrial products, but never in the quantities it used to.

Few Rust Bowl cities escape this industrial decline. The effects reach out all over the nation.

Steel hurts everywhere, from the Monongahela Valley of Pennsylvania, to Birmingham, Alabama. Detroit makes fewer

Blast furnace control room, Brier Hill Works.

The dead hulk of Youngstown Sheet and Tube's Campbell Works.

cars. Fewer miners work in the Mesabi iron range of Minnesota and the coalfields of Appalachia.

Gary, West Virginia, really suffers. Secreted away in the hollows of McDowell County, near the town of Coalwood, it's so remote that it takes two hours of earnest looking down unmarked one-lane roads to find it. The town's bank is located in a house trailer. Our approach is greeted with suspicion by barking dogs. Women, half-hidden by tattered drapes, peer through windows of withering homes. Yellow coal smoke pours from chimneys.

U.S. Steel owns a coal mine here. Some of this coal went to the Youngstown mill where the Marshalls worked. The mine, now closed, supplied coking coal for U.S. Steel blast furnaces all over the Midwest, and employed 1,250 people.

"In Gary holler, we have 90 percent unemployment," mineworker Henry Allen tells us. He points to all the homes down the road from his house. "I'm the only one working on this street. They've shut the mines before, but it's never been like this. If they keep buying Japanese steel, it'll never pick up again."

We ask if the town will perish if the mine doesn't reopen soon.

He raises his eyebrows. "Does a bear shit in the woods?"

A town does not die easy.

At first, the people of Youngstown wait for the mills to reopen. And the companies start gutting them or tearing them down.

The people wait for new business to move into the valley. New business scoffs.

People take matters into their own hands, forming an ecumenical coalition to discuss buying the plants and running them on their own. They fail for many reasons, one being the government will not grant loans. The Feds don't think the plan will work.

Henry Allen, Gary, West Virginia.

Empty homes cannot be sold. Advertisement from the Youngstown *Vindicator*.

The people look to the politicians. But the politicians offer no answers, other than talking about attracting high technology. They plan to spend over $10 million to build a high-tech school, and offer free land.

"How are they going to teach someone like me about something like that?" asks steelworker Platt. "What do I know about computers? A twenty-pound sledgehammer is what I know. I know gears. I don't even know how to play Atari. And maybe 20 percent of the people I worked with in the mill couldn't read or write."

It does not matter anyway. High tech doesn't want Youngstown. Spokesmen for firms like Atari and Hewlett-Packard laugh when asked if their firms would ever build plants anywhere in the Midwest.

Still, many Rust Bowl cities look for high tech to deliver salvation. But as politicians dream of it, high tech is already in trouble. When a firm like Atari moves jobs from California in 1983, does it choose a place like Youngstown? No. It ships jobs to Taiwan and Hong Kong. There's not enough high

Robberies have increased, and store owners are paranoid.

Bankruptcies have increased. Ad from the Youngstown *Vindicator*.

Youngstown skyline,
piles of coking coal,
dead mill, Mahoning
River, and train.

Row of dead storefronts across from the Youngstown Sheet and Tube Works.

tech to go around, anyway. And even if there is, no one knows if it will employ enough people or pay enough in wages to make a difference.

"Do you retrain these people?" asks Dr. John Russo, a labor studies professor at Youngstown State who has charted the death of the town. "Retrain for what? For high tech? That's just another humiliation. People are rolling the dice in terms of their lives."

After five years, only one new major business expressed interest in Youngstown, a blimp factory with a questionable chance of survival. It was only a dream on the drawing boards that appears to be forever shelved. The plant promised to employ thousands in ten years.

Blimps. People laugh. Even if the factory had succeeded, people do not have ten years to wait for jobs.

Meanwhile, Chamber of Commerce representatives and other boosters will argue Youngstown isn't in trouble, that everything is just dandy. The good times will return, they insist.

The boosters cannot be blamed for hiding from the problem. No one seems to have an answer.

So the town dies.

Death does not come quickly. After the first shutdowns, workers have money to spend from severance and unemployment compensation. Families are close, and support each other.

Then the benefits run out. Family relations become strained. The safety net that is supposed to cushion people collapses.

Officials try to measure the cost of human misery in numbers. In the Youngstown area, officials say a peak of 21 percent unemployment was reached. In reality, it was probably closer to 30 percent, because many have been jobless for so long they are no longer counted in statistics, says Professor Russo.

Child abuse rises by 21 percent, say county officials. One mental health clinic reports four thousand calls for help in one month. Suicides climb 70 percent in two years; personal bankruptcies reach two thousand in one year; $1 billion in wages are lost from the plant closings, says Russo. One of every eight people in Mahoning County receives some form of welfare. Up to fifteen hundred people a week visit one Salvation Army soup line. The FBI says the number of burglaries, robberies, and assaults double in the few years following the plant closings, even though the population declines.

Officials and statistics aren't needed to tell you how bad things are, however.

Look at the big men aimlessly walking with their hands in their pockets down the downtown Federal Plaza, where numerous stores are closed. Their sad eyes tell you all you need to know.

Death is reflected in the neighborhoods. Homes are abandoned like so much trash. On Ford Avenue, near the university, over twenty homes are deserted and torn down in a two-year period because so many are fleeing Youngstown. There are few buyers for them. The empty homes are quickly vandalized, windows smashed, mysterious fires set.

The sound of breaking glass interrupts the early morning quiet on Ford Avenue. Neighbors rush from their homes and stand in a semicircle, gawking at the empty Victorian home with its newly broken window. The desperate seller cannot give it away for $10,000. No one speaks, but their eyes express fear. The neighborhood will lose another house, and die just a bit more.

Later this day, smoke fills the sky on the south side of Youngstown. Another abandoned home is ablaze. As flames crackle, firemen stand back, as if gathered around a campfire, and watch it burn until the roof falls in. Not putting it out makes city workers' jobs easier—they already tear down about fifty derelict homes a month. "Arson," is the verdict of one fireman. "At least one house a day burns in this neighborhood."

We ask the then-mayor of Youngstown how he feels about his city burning to the ground. George Vukovich ponders this while sitting in his big chair in City Hall. It is good so many homes are burning, he tells us, because it will force blacks, whom he cites as being responsible for urban decay, to move out of town. Then, says the mayor, we can rebuild. "Through attrition, we're going to eliminate our problems. Youngstown will be one of the most beautiful cities in the nation, in time."

We leave the mayor and walk the streets in a neighborhood of tidy homes that resemble rows of pearly white teeth. Here and there, though, are blackened molars of recently abandoned dwellings. Tiny *stodababbas*, aged ethnic women with heads turbaned in babushkas, hurry from stores to the warmth of their abodes, pressing grocery bags to their breasts. No one seems to mind when we enter the two-story corpse of a home that is a neighbor to two well-manicured bungalows.

A winter breeze invades the zigzag eye socket of a broken upstairs window. The occupants of this forsaken house left in a hurry. Artifacts of the unemployed litter the floor—work clothes, books, letters from a son to his mother.

Dozens of unpaid bills tell a tale of lives shattered like the glass shards strewn at the base of the windows. An overdue electric bill. A gas bill. A dentist bill. All marked "Please pay promptly," they total hundreds of dollars.

The yellowed bills flutter in the wind like crisp, dead leaves.

Down the street, we watch a coughing milk truck pull up to another empty home. Two men pop out and start extracting a supply of plywood, hammers, and saws from the rear.

The death of Youngstown provides a living for Paul Kahkonen and his partner. The two former steelworkers from Washington, Pennsylvania, say they travel a three-state area, boarding homes for the banks when people don't make their mortgage payments.

This three-story home was on their list for today. Kahkonen, wearing a pirate's red bandanna, grasps an armload of tools and walks onto the front porch. A hanging swing looks like a place where lovers once sat. Inside the house, a cupboard is full of canning jars. Books and clothes carpet the floor.

Vandals have preceded them. The walls have been slashed open to get at the copper wire. The thieves, probably unemployed themselves, will sell it for scrap.

"We board up about twenty houses a week," Kahkonen mumbles through a mouthful of nails as he hammers away at a window. "This place gives us a lot of work. This was a nice house. Next week, there won't be anything left. They come and strip everything—siding, pipe, wire. They take them down to the bare studs. This is a crazy town. The first time I came to Youngstown, I couldn't believe it. I never saw anything like this in my whole life.

"It's bad everywhere. We do $100,000 houses. We did a doctor's house in Pittsburgh. In Pittsburgh people are real hostile to us. It's funny. They almost dig us here. We've had some hairy experiences. A few weeks ago, a man came up crying when we went to board his house. They hadn't moved him out. We wouldn't do it. The banks are supposed to guarantee that the people are out.

"I'm just doing my job, see. It just so happens it's not a pleasant job. I have nothing to do with the mortgage companies. It's called hustle. There's no one going to give us work, so we have to hustle. We found a niche to keep working."

Paul Kahkonen inspects a home they had boarded up a few weeks previously. On the side of the house, aluminum siding has been peeled off by vandals who will sell it for scrap.

Dead storefront, which burned down two weeks after this picture was taken.

Street scene, Campbell.

Dead home.

Youngstown is burning to the ground.

The Horvaths.

It doesn't matter that you made mortgage payments on your home for years and always paid your other bills on time. It doesn't matter that you spent twenty-four years designing blueprints for three-thousand-ton presses at Youngstown Steel Door, as Thomas Horvath did. It doesn't matter that you raised three daughters to be successful adults, as Horvath and his wife Luella did.

A lifetime of hard work doesn't buy security, the Horvaths discovered. And so tomorrow, their house is scheduled to be auctioned at the sheriff's foreclosure sale.

In 1978, when the Horvaths both worked, the men in suits from the bank told them the home was worth $55,000, and gave them a $12,000 second mortgage so they could build a swimming pool.

Last week, they sold the house for $44,500, just barely getting out from under a total loss. They feel damn lucky to get that much for it.

"We had a lot of fun here . . . I thought I would die here," says Luella as she packs the last of the kitchenware. "We had $426 monthly payments. We couldn't eat and pay the mortgage. I'm going from a $60,000 house to a $6,000 trailer. We'll clear just enough to pay for the trailer. But we're not unhappy. A lot of people are worse off. At least we have a place."

Both swig beers. Thomas, one of seventeen hundred workers laid off at Steel Door, burrows his balding head into a box, packing away a sign with their name on it that hung at the entrance to the swimming pool. "At least I'll have something to remember it by. Hell. I've got to start from scratch at forty-three years old."

Luella finishes a beer and cracks another. The couple sits at the kitchen table, the only remaining furniture. We leave them staring in silence at the bare walls of the home where they spent a lot of Christmases with their daughters.

Moving day. The Horvaths sit on their front steps for the last time.

A monument of an open-hearth furnace built to honor steelworkers on Federal Plaza, downtown Youngstown. Residents have vandalized the sculpture. They hate it because it reminds them of the good days. In the background, a store advertises it is going out of business.

Street scene, downtown Youngstown, on Federal Plaza.

Civic pride remains strong.

Union headquarters at Lordstown, where a General Motors assembly plant is located, near Youngstown.

Mounds of coking coal for steel-making pile up south of downtown, the product of some of the last coking furnaces that closed just after the picture was taken.

Sheriff's foreclosure sale at the courthouse.

The pounding of a gavel resounds through the cavernous lobby of the musty marble courthouse. It's time to begin the sheriff's foreclosure sale. Thirty or so bankers and others crowd around the auctioneer standing at a lecturn. Ed Mann, the former president of the United Steelworkers of America Local 1462, at the Brier Hill Works, has come to watch. After the auctioneer announces the withdrawl of the Horvath home from the list, bids start on a $100,000 home in suburban Boardman.

"This is people's property!" Mann pleads. "You're ruining people's lives!"

The bankers ignore Mann's shouting. The attorney for the bank bids successfully at $66,000. He turns to a very obese banker, who bears a frightening resemblance to the pitiless fat-cat cliché we all dread. He has his script down pat. The fat man turns to the attorney and whispers, "We'll evict them right away."

Then a home is sold for $6,000. This banker, much younger and seemingly more compassionate, explains the bank has $18,000 in the house. "We're losing $12,000," he says. "It'll probably be torn down."

"These are people who did everything right," says Mann, back at his modest home. "They went to college. They went to church. They bought into the system. Now what? This is a depression. You used to be able to live the American Dream. With corporations, it's all 'Gimme, gimme, gimme.' They want a profit *now*. They don't care about people.

"Can a country grow and be healthy with this going on? Let's stop all the bullshit and get money into people's hands so we can get the country moving. If they didn't make one nuclear submarine, they could put Youngstown back to work.

"We're wasting people. There are people here who are twenty-six years old and have never held a job. The schools aren't doing anything. People in their twenties and thirties are feeling they have no sense of self-worth. It consumes you when you stand in line day after day. This country is fucked up."

Job line.

Chapter 3: **MOVING ON**

One thousand shadowy figures silently perform an impromptu dance in the middle of the darkened forest, an exercise meant to ward off the sting of wind shrieking across endless frozen fields of corn stubble. Three in the morning is not a pleasant hour to find yourself outdoors in the late Ohio winter.

The shivering snake of humanity loops in a line for one-quarter mile through a grove of shagbark hickories. Those dressed for looks suffer the most, wheezing and muttering under steamy breath as they stamp the frozen ground. The smart ones huddle in sleeping bags or wear deer hunting duds. One woman clutches a whining baby. Another with her eyes closed grasps a Bible. Their faces tell their stories— they have not been recently visited by smiles. Two thousand sunken eyes stare blankly at a blinding 400-watt bulb burning over the door of a building.

They have come because at 8 A.M., men inside that building will allow them to do something they hardly ever get a chance at anymore: fill out a job application.

There are two hundred jobs open at a factory in the town of Clyde. The jobs exist because the company permanently closed a sister plant in Michigan. This is the second of three days the firm would accept applications. Yesterday, four thousand others showed up. Word of the jobs spread far. Some have journeyed from Kentucky, Michigan, and West Virginia.

Babies cry. Muted coughs rat-a-tat. Otherwise, the line is hushed.

Then, three newcomers approach, dragging a fifty-gallon steel barrel containing a blazing fire.

Screams fill the air. A shrunken old woman hunkered beneath a handwoven shawl waves her fist and spits obscenities. A man from the front of the line comes down and explains to the trio the police announced that if anyone is caught making a fire, the whole bunch of them will be thrown out. Cops didn't want fires, because yesterday's crowd was tearing down buildings for fuel. The fire carriers, who knead their hands over the mouth of the drum, refuse to extinguish the blaze.

The man returns to his place and holds council with his friends. A group of men with fight in their eyes march back down.

"Get that fire out of here, asshole!" snarls the clench-fisted leader. "We aren't getting kicked out for nobody!" The mob grabs the barrel and heaves it over. A shower of sparks illuminates the men, and the rest of the line applauds.

"We won't kick your ass. We'll kill anybody who gets us kicked out," warns one of the men in a low voice, who says it as if he means it.

A round of congratulations greet the men when they return to the head of the line. The focus of their anger is gone, but feelings run high and they shout into the night.

"Harold B. says Reagan can take food stamps and shove them up his ass!"

"John A. says Reagan can keep welfare . . . just give me a job!"

"If they put me behind a broom, I push it for three dollars an hour. I got to support my kids. I sold all my shit. I don't got nothing else!" hollers another.

Chances for landing one of the jobs are grim, those nearest the door agree.

"I figure it's like trying to spit into an empty pool to fill it. That's the chance I have of getting a job here. But it's a chance," says Bill Carver, a jobless machinist who must support three children.

"In two and a half months, my unemployment runs out," Carver continues, adjusting the thick watch cap covering his short-cropped hair, a holdover from his days in the service. "How am I going to live? I'm wearing 1974 Army-issue boots. When they wear out, I'm going to have to patch them. I shoot me deer. I shoot me rabbit. And now that it should be getting warm, I'll fish. I'm smart. I'll eat. But what about these other people?"

By first light, almost two thousand applicants are present. The line has lengthened to the street, blocking traffic. Sheriff's deputies decide to move it.

A big mistake.

The move starts orderly enough. The crowd, however, takes on a mind of its own. Looks on nervous faces say, Will I lose my place? That son of a bitch will get ahead of me! No way!

At once, a swarming Oklahoma land rush of cold, tired, angry job-seekers break loose in a full-tilt run, out of control and mad to be the first near that door, dragging bouncing children, lawn chairs, blankets.

The deputies wisely flee for cover. It's terribly frightening to see two thousand desperate people running at you. People like this are capable of anything.

The mob streams around us. Some laugh crazily; others are on the verge of tears. A girl wearing a delicate flower dress trips near me, sprawling in the dirt. A woman leaps over her body, shouting, "I'll outrun them all! No one's getting ahead of me!" I dodge people and bend to help the girl, but she is off and running before I get close.

The race stops of its own accord. No one is seriously hurt. The doors open and small groups are allowed inside to warm their hands from nine hours of cold and fill out applications. Most are polite, and answer with loud "Yes, sirs!" to interviewers.

Company officials say four people will process the thousands of applications in the next few days.

Carver exits.

"This is a last chance for me. When my unemployment runs out, I go south. If I don't get a job or have money, at least I'll be warm. I call this the 1980s Depression."

Snow begins falling. He shoves his hands in his pockets and wanders off, disappearing in the mist.

Fires weren't allowed,
but some brought them.

When deputies move the line, job seekers break loose in a full-tilt run.

The race stops of its own accord, and people wait their turn to fill out applications.

Inside, filling out applications.

Veronica Lukas grew up in the "bad" part of Youngstown, with everything against her. She is poor and black.

Patricia Schultz grew up in the "good" part of town, with everything in her favor. She is well-to-do and white.

Both share a common destiny—the right to no future. The sour economy has brought equality to Youngstown.

We talk to Schultz at the vast, tree-lined campus of the high school in suburban Boardman.

"I have no future here," says Schultz. "A lot of families who were close aren't any more. I saw my dad go through hell when he lost his job. My dad did a lot for that company. There's a lot of drinking and drugs among kids. I regret my teenage years. I'm leaving as soon as I get out."

Across town at a southside community center where youths have gathered to apply for temporary, part-time, subsidized summer jobs, Veronica Lukas waits with hundreds of others in line.

"My brother is out of work. My sister was laid off last summer. My father was laid off two years ago," says Lukas. "I'm leaving, going to California. I'd be real happy with a restaurant job."

Folks grow weary of standing in lines. Job lines. Soup lines. Unemployment lines. Welfare lines.

They have one too many doors slammed in their face when they look for work.

They tire of fighting with their spouses.

They rebel at the agony of months of sleeping in late and drinking into the night.

Idleness is a disease for which the only cure is action.

Gotta go . . . gotta go . . . gotta do something, some of them say.

So they pack the old Chevy. Catch a bus. Hold out a thumb. Even hop a freight train.

Hit the road.

Says Stan, a metalworker: "Look, it's a depression here. I feel like I'm useless. You get nervous and crazy. I don't know where to turn. I've got four kids. House payments. I've got 110,000 miles on the car, and it's broke-down. When I get it going, I'm going."

Says Liddy, a steel salesman: "Lots of my friends have blown town. I've got 140 résumés out, and nothing is happening. I won't stand in a welfare line. And my savings are gone. So I'm going to give it a shot and get out of here."

You ask the fleeing people where they're going. Place names roll off their tongues in a tone of voice usually reserved for speaking to a lover.

Texas . . . Colorado . . . California.

That's where the jobs are, they say. "California is it," says one Youngstowner. "I'm going to kiss the ground when I get there."

Interstate 80 is *the* road out of Youngstown. The jobless travel it, or other distant highways, such as Interstates 70, 40, and 10. Cities along these routes like St. Louis add their own tide of jobless to the road.

It is night when we leave Youngstown behind, heading down the unfolding blacktop pathway, the yellow brick road, looking for the ruby in the eye of the wizard.

Chapter 4: **THE GATEWAY CITY**

A pitiless drizzle pockmarks the skin of the Mississippi, gorged with runoff bled from the backside of the whole middle part of the country, water rich and brown in color as Indiana bottomland. A chain dance of traffic snarls on Interstates 70 and 44, the modern-day equivalent of Route 66. A cheerless city, gray like the sky, appears through the rain-spattered car windows. St. Louis is the first real stop for anyone using this route to escape the industrial heartland.

Soon it will be dark. Night promises to be ghastly for any creature unfortunate enough to be caught outdoors. Pigeons, rats, and other urban beasts sequester themselves in forgotten dank nooks—the same holes of refuge sought by the hitchhikers, homeguards, and hoboes. These men and women without homes hurry to bivouac under bridges, walking shoulder-to-shoulder down sidewalks populated with business people on their way back to the suburbs.

At a swank store near Memorial Plaza, Don crouches from the deluge in the foyer. He tucks his racquetball racquet under his arm and rubs his ears to keep warm. Men in suits and women in dresses looking at him could think he's a college student waiting for a bus. They might not even notice him; he doesn't look much different than any young up-and-coming guy with a successful future lying ahead. In fact,

trade his casual clothes for one of those suits, and he'd be a Xerox copy of any one of them. He's proper and refined down to his toes; even his posture shows he's run in business circles.

Yes, he's just like them. But he is trembling from fear and cold, and they are not.

He has no idea what to do. Last night, his first on the street, he managed to sleep on the floor of the bus station until police evicted him with a warning never to return. Thoughts of suicide fill his mind. He's already tried that twice since he hit bottom, and failed. Next time, he wants to succeed.

Not so long ago, Don had it made. He was the envy of his peers. And why not? At the age of twenty-eight he had his own small cleaning business with a crew of workers, a house, three children.

He cannot believe how fast his life was turned upside down. When the recession dragged on, he lost his biggest account. Then, the business went bankrupt. He lost the house. His wife was angry that Don would not get welfare to avoid total economic collapse. He was too proud. I'll find work, he kept telling her. But no one would hire him. Marital problems ensued. His wife and children moved home with her mother.

Don went back to his parents' farm in Illinois. For nine months he looked for work, often standing in job lines each day with hundreds of other men. Finally, the pressure and humiliation became too much. Last week, he bought a one-way Amtrak ticket here, got a cheap hotel room, and began looking for work. Two days ago, his money ran out.

As Don jingles the last fifty-eight cents in his pocket, the store manager opens the door and tersely informs him vagrants aren't allowed to loiter in front of the building.

Vagrant? Don wants to scream. He wants to say, *I used to shop here. I'm no bum! I had it made! Don't you remember?*

Nothing comes from his mouth, though. He can't speak through choking tears. He runs into the downpour, sobbing.

Four blocks away, a tall man knocks at the locked door of a mission. It's five minutes to nine. No one answers. The man paces, continuing his knocking. "This is a rough town to find work," he pronounces. "And a rough town to be on the streets after dark."

Fifteen minutes pass. Finally, a mission worker comes to the door. "You're ten minutes too late, brother. We stopped taking people in at nine," he says, even though there is plenty of room. The tall man explains he was here before the deadline. "We have no way of knowing that. The rules are the rules," says the worker. The man begs—to no avail. The door slams in his face.

Pure outrage erupts. He pummels the door. "You call yourselves Christians? Christians, shit!"

The mission responds by calling the police. As the tall man runs off, a streamliner with no belongings other than the clothes on his body shows up. He too is denied a bed. The policeman arrives.

"I ain't got nothing. Where do I go? Where do I go?" he asks the cop. The cop warns he might get arrested if he sleeps in the bus station, and suggests an abandoned building. There are dozens of the cavelike shells in the neighborhood.

"Every night, this place calls us," the cop whispers to us. "I don't know what they do in there. They sure don't help people."

The streamliner goes off in the rain. The mission worker shouts after him, "God bless you, brother."

The next night, over at the Sally, Don straggles in carrying his racquetball racquet and an Adidas bag. Clean-shaven and with some life left in his darkened eyes, he stands out in stark contrast to the junkyard of humanity hidden in the shadows of the basement. Someone on the street told him about the mission, so he came yesterday. It was the only thing to do.

All of us are ushered into the sweltering chapel for the evening's earbanging.

A haggard, humorless woman claws at an out-of-tune piano. The self-appointed preacher, a bargain-basement Billy Graham, launches into a tirade, while a backup preacher wearing Coke-bottle glasses claps and chants.

You are evil sinners, nothing but worthless, inferior alcoholics, goes his line. He doesn't account for those who may be here only because they're unemployed. He seems to delight in putting the men down. He sings "What a friend you have in Jesus," in a cracking voice. "God! God! God! Love! Love! Love!" he whines over and over, shaking. The apprentice Jesus salesman yowls with his nose pitched in the air, sweat showering off his forehead.

Homeguards, local winos who are regulars here, have heard this spiel a hundred times. They sprawl in the chairs, snoring. Don buries his head in his thin hands.

After an hour, it ends. Homeguards who know how to play the game wake up in time to come forward and "take"

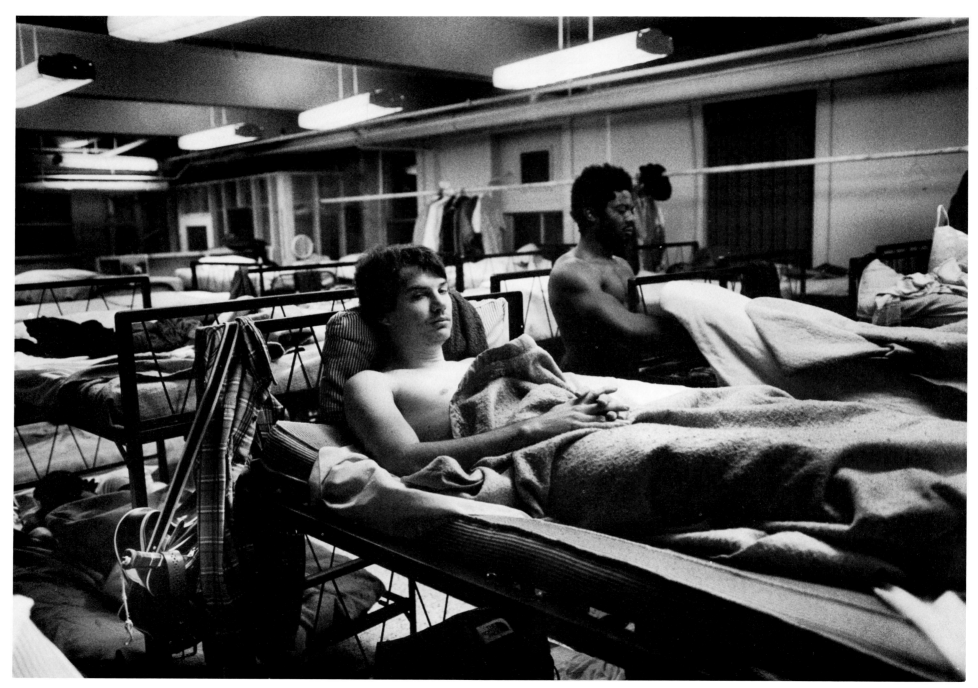

Don in bed at the St. Louis Sally.

Jesus in their hearts. They're rewarded by being allowed to eat first.

Don passes on dinner and slumps on a sagging bunk bed, one of many lined up in rows, much like a prison gang cell. We're lorded over by a cruel wino, perched in a glass booth, who delights in barking orders for us to lie in our bunks. (Many missions put "reformed" homeguards in charge. There's nothing meaner than a wino given authority after years of abuse on the streets.)

It's been a long time since Don has found someone to talk with. From his bed, he dumps his story on us with the speed of an AM radio disk jockey.

"I want to ask that preacher, What happened to the Parthians in the sixth century, sucker. They act so much better than you. They treat you like a dog.

"Last night was my first. It was culture shock. I feel like I've stepped into Bangladesh. I grew up having everything. We grew up in the fifties and sixties. We had all the good things. I thought poor meant you didn't want a job. We survived Vietnam. Race riots. Nixon. And now this. People are becoming accustomed to fifteen percent unemployment! That's terrible. It's one thing to be poor and stay poor. It's another thing to be middle class and go down. It hurts like a son of a bitch.

"I feel like I'm suffocating more each day. There I was. Joe College. Friends I went to high school with made fun of me because I went to college and graduated. But when things were good, I was looked up to. All I ever wanted was to have a business. I was proud as a peacock. By the time I went down, my neighbors were out of work, too. One guy got down and left his family. And this was suburbia! I had eight thousand dollars in the bank. That's bubble gum when it starts going."

The lights go out, but beams stream into the bed area from a bulb in the glass booth, creating harsh shadows.

Don's head resting on a pillow is outlined by that dim glow; his mouth never stops moving—it resembles the flapping, gaping beak of a baby bird begging food from its mother.

"You get a feeling from relatives . . . like when are you going to get a job? They don't say that, but you feel it. You feel like an idiot. Every meal you get for free from them, that feeling builds. I'd stand in line for five hours to apply for a minimum-wage job. When I'd get home, everyone asked how I did in the interview. They said I was a great guy and had lots of experience and that I should get the job. They didn't understand. I was one of dozens. I spent maybe two minutes with the interviewer. That weighed me down. That makes you feel you have to leave."

He sobs, the tears flowing down his face. Men snore around him. Don clenches his fists and shakes his hands in the air.

"I tried to kill myself, by taking pills. They saved me. When I came to, I regretted that. When I took the pills, I felt relieved. I had no emotions. The next day, I read in the paper that the recession is over. That was great. Everyone else is making it, and I'm not.

"It's like a knife gouging through your gut. I tried to sell my blood today. I'd never done that before. They told me my blood pressure was too high and they couldn't take me. It was because I was scared. I never had high blood pressure before in my life. They would have paid me seven dollars. It's unbelievable what seven dollars can mean. It sounded like gold to me.

"I thought of stealing food today. That scared me. The only thing I ever stole before was a piece of candy when I was a kid. You can sit in a university like I did and talk about the poor. You can speculate what you'd do. But hunger reduces all variables. Hunger will make you do anything.

"It's scary to look at that guy (he points to a shriveled wino two beds away) and feel you're going that way. It's a

Don waiting to sell blood plasma for the first time in his life, St. Louis.

panic thing. If I can get one little job, it will bring me back.

"I carry my racquetball racquet because it makes me invisible. People think I'm a college student, that I belong, that I'm part of society. It's the only thing that keeps me from going over the edge.

"I rode around on the bus all day today. It takes up a lot of time. When I got off the bus, I cried. It was the only thing that was familiar to me. The bus became human. It was the only friend I had. And it left me.

"A guy tried to talk me into hopping a train to Tampa this morning, but I'm thinking of Denver. I keep hearing there's lots of jobs there. Hitchhiking is bad. They know you're desperate. They know you're hungry. They're afraid

of that. I hit the road. It was probably an immature thing to do, but I had to do it. I'd rather be like a whale who goes off to beach himself—you know how some whales do that. I'd rather go down alone. I don't want people to see me like this. I wish I could humble myself down and accept this."

Don pulls a blanket over his head, but tosses and turns sleeplessly. Each move prompts loud squeals from the ancient springs of the rusting army bunk. Real sleep is impossible. Gasping, hacking old men, steamy heat, and the stench of stale wine breath see to that.

Five A.M. comes too soon. The mean wino clicks on the lights. "Time to run, gentlemen," he chuckles, throwing us out into darkness.

Don looks out at rail yards from top of Gateway Arch, St. Louis.

Chapter 5: **INTO THE JUNGLE**

Don's heart pounds as he races along the railroad tracks, his long legs windmilling beneath him. He's still not running fast enough. He mouths the words "I can't make it," but the utterance is erased by an explosion of sound an arm's length to our left.

Five idling Missouri Pacific units tower over us, their throaty voices grumbling in the gathering gloom. Power. Each firing piston detonates like a grenade, the shots blending together to form a shrill symphony, shuddering the ground.

Behind the units, a three-quarter-mile-long freight train waits to pull out of the yard on the main line. Destination: Kansas City. Then, on to Pueblo, south of Denver.

The diesels buck and groan, "snapping" the train. A resonant *boom* echoes across the yard as the knuckles stretch and set the cars in motion.

Don panics. The last train of the day is leaving and he's not on it. No way does he want to spend another night in the mission.

Grasping his chest for breath, Don reaches the first of the cars rumbling past at a spanking pace. He jogs along with it, afraid to touch the ladder. Images of his legs being sliced off by the wheels—churning like rotary razors only a foot away—flash through his mind. His hands snag a rung.

Still running, his legs leave the gravel, and in one quick motion, he is aboard, gasping on the floor of an empty three-level railcar designed to carry automobiles.

A switchman who observes us shouts, "Watch the main yard in KC! It's hot! The bull's been throwing everyone in jail!"

The sympathetic worker's warning trails off as the train picks up speed and leaves the yard. Gripping an outside ladder tightly, Don scales it to the roof, trying not to look at the blurred ground in the space between the cars.

Behind, the sixty-three-story Gateway Arch—erected to commemorate St. Louis's role in history as the entrance to the West for the pioneers—dominates the evening skyline. Below the arch lies Busch Stadium, packed with thousands of spectators for the rained-out second game of the season between the Cardinals and the Pittsburgh Pirates.

"Goodbye, St. Louis!" Don hollers. He jumps up and down, shaking his fist. "Good riddance! No regrets! I can starve here or in Denver!"

Don falls silent, then squats like a meditating monk. The arch disappears. We are in the country, dashing through a black forest of trees yet to be clothed in leaves. Wind whisks past his ears, a misting rain falls, yet the new hobo remains immobile. With the coming of full darkness and serious

On the roof of the automobile carrier as the train pulls out of the St. Louis Missouri Pacific yard, St. Louis.

On the roof of the railcar, as the Gateway Arch disappears in the background.

Sign near Union Pacific rail yard, Kansas City.

rainfall, we clamor back to the shelter of the first level, munching on a dinner of Spam and crackers.

Riding a freight train is not a genteel experience. Trains are inherently smutty. Don quickly finds himself thoroughly soiled with an oily scum that's soaked into his pores. The suspension is designed for cargo, not human flesh. The bucking floor spits him about like a droplet of water falling in a pan of smoking grease. Reverberating clangs drown out voices as the walls rattle and vibrate, a sound that can only be likened to finding yourself stuffed in a garbage can being hammered with a baseball bat by a rampaging gorilla. Don tries to urinate. The raging wind douses him with piss.

Don starts cackling. He laughs until his sides hurt, and then some more. It's the first time he's laughed in weeks. We laugh with him. This is just too brutal. He rubs his eyes with filthy hands, turning them into two white spots surrounded by blackened rings.

"Believe it or not, this is a lot better than the mission," he yells as he crawls in a secondhand sleeping bag, oblivious to the maelstrom. The bag is needed to repel the glacial gale. Bulls tell of finding unprepared new-time hoboes dead from exposure in boxcars when trains enter yards after long trips.

Don is on an important train. Lesser trains side for the hotshot, allowing it to pass. The power of the train seems to have affected Don. He draws from it and appears to be rising from the abyss.

The train screws it on, highballing at sixty miles an hour through the Ozark Mountain night, down the aisle of steel, carrying its secret passenger toward an uncertain future.

Three A.M., the Kansas City Mopac (Missouri Pacific) rail yard:

As when it started, the train creaks to a halt with a loud bang. That's followed by a *whoosh* when the train drops the air from its brakes. Don's legs crumple uselessly beneath him as he hits the hoarfrost-covered ground. The legs are bone-cold and simply refuse to function.

Disoriented in the sprawling yard full of hundreds of sleeping trains, Don staggers to a switchman for advice. Most yard workers hate the bulls as much as hoboes and are usually downright helpful.

The yard worker tells Don our train will not go on to Colorado, but will be broken into pieces that will travel in all directions. He warns Don that the bull threw two men in jail yesterday after he found them on a train, and that we'd better watch ourselves.

We hurry from the yard. Don clutches the racquetball racquet in one hand and his bedroll in the other. He curls up and shivers in a frozen ditch, waiting for sunrise.

Daylight finds us walking through a swamp south of the yard, toward an abandoned grain elevator surrounded by a thicket of woods. Don wants a safe place to hide from the bull while he plots his next move. The yard worker told him it will be at least one day before a train leaves for Pueblo.

The sun does little to warm him and rid his body of stiffness. Sleep was impossible. His sleeping bag was designed for kinder climates. His eyes burn and each cough sends out a cloud of steamy breath.

Don's on home turf. As a child, he spent a lot of time playing around grain elevators on his parents' farm. He may not understand street life or freight trains, but grain elevators, he knows.

The imposing cement monument has been abandoned for years. Don pushes aside some brush, only to find all the doors and windows sealed shut.

Enterprising vandals have chiseled torso-size entrance

holes, however. Don squirms through one like a lizard, climbing an interior ladder to the cramped third-floor level of the ten-story structure.

"What a blessing—a floor that's not moving!" Don exclaims, rubbing his sore buttocks. It seems to be a pretty weird dream: living in an Oz-like forgotten grain elevator in Kansas City!

Throughout the day, we cozy up our new home. The surroundings remind us of a scene of a bombed-out church in a low-budget World War II movie. We sweep the cubicle of fossilized, rotted grain and bat droppings; haul up gear and firewood through the window with a rope; nap.

As the sun sets over Kansas, Don perches himself in the window of the concrete aerie overlooking the Mopac yard, watching the advance of shadows. He produces pictures of his kids, aged two, three, and five.

"I'd work in the bottom of a salt mine to get them back. If I can ride one of those suckers across the country, I can do anything," he sighs, pointing to the freight yard.

"Eighty percent of the people I know couldn't imagine me here. They think I'm a soft guy. But I'm a competitor. I'm good at racquetball. I've played sports all my life, and I know when I'm behind in the game. I'm behind now. But I'm starting to feel I'm going to score. Since I hopped that train, things have changed. I feel like I can do it. I've got a feeling about Denver."

The sun vanishes. We kindle the fire. Don lounges in the chamber illuminated and warmed by the blaze. Supper is quickly slurped from a tin can of soup, bought with money earned from selling blood plasma the day he left St. Louis. They finally accepted him at the blood bank the second day he tried, and Don was thankful. Instead of working for a living, Don bleeds for a living. He smirks at this observation. The seven dollars he was paid for a pint of his blood is half the amount he would have earned in a good economy. Because so many of the unemployed want to sell plasma, there is an oversupply, and prices have dropped accordingly.

Railcars bang and squeal in the hump yard as workers build new trains, forlorn music accompanied by a chorus of thousands of crooning swamp frogs.

Sleep comes quickly, and is good.

It's tough to freight out of a hot yard. The challenge appeals to Don's competitive edge. This is the racquetball game of life—and he wants to win.

The first step toward victory will be to beat that bull and ride out of his yard.

It begins with an early morning reconnaissance trip into the forbidden yard. We find a wooded area out of sight of the yard towers where the trainmaster sits, sometimes accompanied by the bull. We draw straws. Don and Mike lose, and thus are elected for the foray. I tell them to enjoy themselves in jail if they get caught. I recline on the packs and watch them cross an open area. They place a bridge pillar between themselves and one of the towers. Only then do they jog into the heart of the yard. They slink down narrow corridors between boxcars that seem to stretch for miles, until they find yard worker.

Track three, sometime this afternoon, is the official word.

They steal back and we wait. And wait. And wait. Most hoboes spend more time waiting for trains than actually riding them, Don learns.

At least six years later, it seems, a switch engine begins building a train on the proper track. There are no empty boxcars. An unprotected grainer is out of the question, as snow threatens. The only ride visible is on a car carrier loaded with small pickup trucks. We take it.

Coffee, inside grain elevator.

We move into the abandoned grain elevator, Kansas City, with Don guiding the packs up.

The train sits motionless for an hour, waiting for the units to hook up.

Bulls are especially picky about hoboes riding full automobile carriers. Some unscrupulous hoboes will tamper with the cars, and bulls assume most tramps are not as honorable as Don. Hoboes on such railcars have really got to watch it. So when we hear approaching footsteps, we plaster ourselves to the floor of one of the truck beds.

The unseen visitor jumps on the car carrier in front of this one. Don's eyes widen. Feet thudding on the gravel signal the approach of our unknown investigator. Crunch, crunch, crunch. Metal clangs as the feet reach our carrier.

Don holds his breath and closes his eyes.

Silence. Whomever it is stands thirty feet from us, scanning the inside of this carrier. The feet land back on the stones, walking off.

Don sits up. Was it the bull? He doesn't know and doesn't care to find out.

The blast from the diesels' horns pierce the silence of the Great Plains as the train barrels across Kansas through a raging blizzard. Don cocoons himself in the truck bed—the cab is locked—but the wet snow finds a way to swirl inside the car carrier and land on him.

Hunger bites his stomach. All the food has long since been eaten. For something to do, the jobless refugee peeks like a spy through a crack in the wall. Timeless prairie scenery sweeps past.

In a tiny cottage, he sees a woman cooking dinner. In a town, kids gawk at the train with the amazed look kids always seem to have for things big and powerful. At a rail crossing, a weary couple sits in a tired old truck, impatiently waiting for the train to pass. The *ding-ding-ding* of the crossing gate drones by. In open country, snow settles thickly on fields of red winter wheat.

Don tires of sightseeing and slumps in the bed of the Ford pickup destined for a dealer's showroom in San Francisco.

I walk to the front of the railcar, watching the river of ground rush beneath my feet. Snow stings my eyes. I look back at Don hiding in the burrow of his sleeping bag.

What fate awaits him in Denver? Without money, how will he get an address and stay clean so he can get a job? Who wants to hire an out-of-town "bum"? Is he destined to live in this world where he does not belong? Will he wind up like Alabama?

Thomas Jefferson "Alabama" Glenn was an old-time hobo who spent his life on the rails. He was known in every West Coast jungle by his snowy beard as wild as ragweed, his two missing thumbs, his good humor, and the way he shook from Parkinson's disease. He started rail riding just after the Great Depression, and he was scarred by the Depression as everyone was who lived through it.

I first met Alabama in the Sacramento yards. During several encounters when I was first learning about hobo life, he taught me much about the fine art of working a yard; making a good camp; how to pick food from dumpsters; and generally avoid trouble. He showed old hobo tricks, like how to boil coffee water when there is no wood for a fire, or when you lack a pot, using nothing more than a discarded wine bottle and some shredded paper. You fill the bottle with water to its brim, mound paper around it, and set it afire. In minutes, the water is steaming.

Eating out of dumpsters sounds disgusting, but a McDonald's hamburger thrown in a trash bin because it was too old to sell does not taste bad after you have gone days without food. New-timers discover what Alabama has long known: the $70 monthly government stipend for "stamps," as food stamps are called on the street, does not last long.

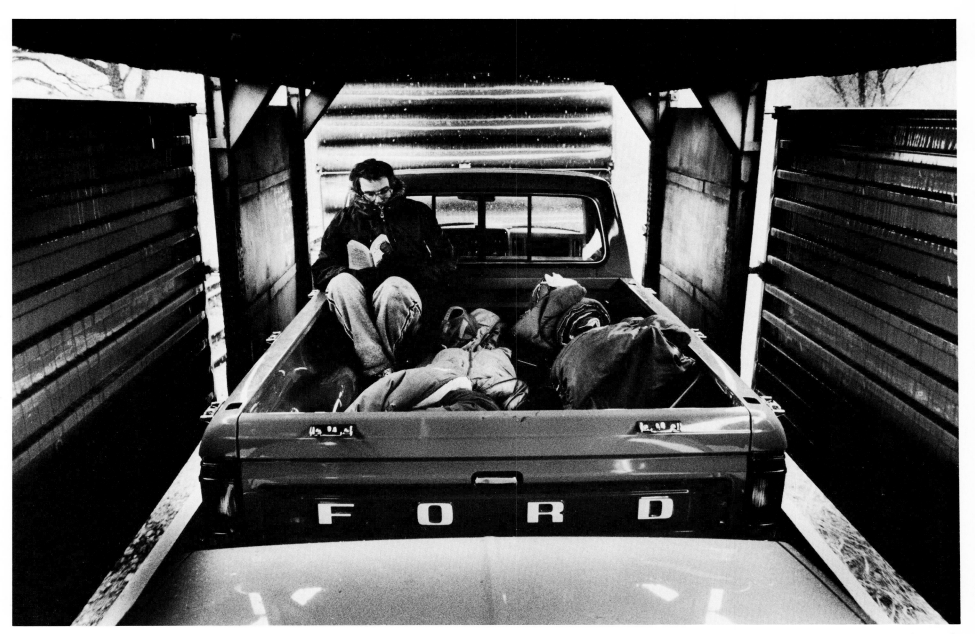

On the train from Kansas City to Pueblo, Colorado. Snow swirls inside.

Who can eat on just over two bucks a day? And because of crackdowns, both new-timers and old-timers cannot always get stamps.

Only a stupid man could starve or die of exposure out here, however, said Alabama. He continually lectured his number-one rule of survival, learned after almost forty years of rail riding: Never cross anyone.

"I can walk into any jungle and I don't have to worry," he said while squatting on the floor of a dead boxcar, eating a taco I'd brought him. Between bites, he confided he wanted to stop tramping, though, because he increasingly feared an ill-breed of hobo he has seen since the economy went bad. You must dread these crazies, he warned. It's gotten dangerous out here.

His home of the moment was the boxcar. The smell of urine dominated. Bottles of white port with 99-cent price tags decorated the grounds, accompanied by spent cans of Vienna sausage; socks blackened and soaked with grease and creosote; sheaves of yellowed newspapers. The whole mess baked in 100-degree heat.

It's hard to imagine how Alabama lived this way for so long. It showed on his face. Dirt was tattooed in the grooves of his wrinkles. His main concerns were food and shelter. He walked hunched, like a woods creature. Alabama was part beast.

Not long after my last talk with Alabama, we caught a Burlington Northern north to Oregon. We returned to California on the Southern Pacific. About ten miles from the big Roseville yard, our train was sided for a northbound.

An open boxcar on the approaching train flashed past. Standing in the doorway was Alabama. He started whooping hellos, cheering and waving as he hung by one arm out the door. He continued waving until he became a mere speck that soon disappeared from sight.

That's the last time we saw him.

Twelve weeks later, he was dead, murdered with two other hoboes in the Oroville jungle.

His body was found by a hobo in the shade of two stunted walnut trees in a parched, wind-whipped field of star thistle, next to the tracks. Also dead were Wade Southern, forty-six, and Bernard Moseley, fifty-one. Southern and Moseley were shot, and all three had been repeatedly stabbed—sometime during the night while they sat around a fire. There was no sign of a struggle. Oroville police say robbery was not a motive. Police suspect a fellow transient who would "kill for the sake of killing" may be responsible. A "crazy." It was sobering and sad news.

Killers on the rails.

In the following year, we heard of deaths everywhere. In Spokane, Washington, a hobo was stabbed to death and another seriously wounded by gunfire. Rumors circulated about hoboes being thrown out of speeding boxcars near Salt Lake City. In Yuma, Arizona, the bull told of two young men beaten bloody until dead while they dozed in their sleeping bags. Two murders occurred in the Klamath Falls jungle. A murder in Tucson.

Three weeks after Alabama's death, we had occasion to ride a freight from Sacramento to Salt Lake City, and beyond to Denver. In Oroville, we had had a ten-minute delay while workers changed crews. We sat in a nice boxcar, our feet dangling over the edge.

Two men who we'd earlier seen kissing approached, wanting to ride with us. Not more than a thousand feet away was the clump of trees where Alabama was murdered. Alabama said never let anyone you don't trust in your boxcar, especially over the mountains at night.

We declined their company. As fast as we said no, one pulled a gun. "You want problem?" he asked. They jumped on. We jumped off and ran as fast as we could.

Four days later, when we got to Denver, a man who was

You can run into bad characters on the rails. Guns are now displayed openly. Western Pacific yard, Sacramento.

sniffing glue attacked me in the jungle, wielding a wire with which he wanted to strangle me. I escaped by climbing a bridge piling. I was ready to fend him off with rocks, when Mike and two new-timers we were riding with returned, scaring him away.

Anyone who rides the rails for any length of time is playing the odds. Sooner or later, you will run into a crazy. You can try reasoning with them, but that won't always work. It is wise to carry a club and a knife, at the minimum, for protection.

New-timers like Don could be damned to wind up like Alabama if they live out here for long. After every war and economic crisis, there have been men so mentally wounded they've said to hell with it, and joined the permanent roster of outcasts who never stop riding the rails or living on the streets. It's happened from the Civil War to Vietnam, from the Depression of the late 1800s to the Depression of the 1930s.

Of course, many come out of the downward spiral, such as John Anderson. It was June 1934, the peak of the Great Depression, when Anderson left his small South Dakota hometown and went on the tramp for one summer, hunting work. Bulls were tough, he recalled, missions lousy, home was under bridges or in boxcars, and rumors of cities full of jobs abounded.

"You'd hear of farm work or something going on somewhere, and you'd make a mad dash for a freight train and hope you'd get there before everyone else. That's what kept you moving. When you got there, it was just as bad as the place you came from."

He came out of it and eventually did well. "It's happening again," he says. He worries it may not end up good for many people this time.

Which way will Don go? If he gets a break, he'll wind up

It's against the law to ride freights. This sign was put up in the Western Pacific yard in Oroville after Alabama was murdered.

like Anderson. If he doesn't, the streets might chew him up. A guy like Don is fodder out here.

I return to the bed of my pickup and sleep.

"Just get in?" an unemployed machinist from Lima, Ohio, asks Don. "So did we. If we don't find anything here, we're heading for California."

The group of men call out a litany of home towns from Florida to Michigan. All have just hitchhiked here to Denver on a job hunt.

Don stammers, but doesn't finish a sentence. He hasn't been downtown more than five minutes, and everywhere he sees job-hungry men with backpacks. There are more people looking for work here than in St. Louis! Everyone back in the Midwest said this was the place to go. His hopes of Denver being a job-hunting mecca are evaporating.

The final leg of the ordeal was too much. The train sided often, taking nineteen hours to arrive in Pueblo from Kansas City. It was a worse ride than the first, a veritable freezer and food blender on wheels. Then, when we hitchhiked north to Denver, we were picked up by a drunken man who wanted sex. He drove us down a dirt road, frightening us, but took us to Denver after his advances were declined.

Don is dizzy. He grasps his head, quickstepping away from the group of fellow job seekers. He feels he'll never work again.

More snow threatens to fall from nasty clouds racing like gangs of thugs over the Front Range of the Rockies. We board a bus, waving farewell to Don. His face is so full of uncertainty, but he's seemingly a stronger man than the one we'd found in the St. Louis mission. He stands alone on a street corner, empty-handed. He's thrown away the racquetball racquet.

Don reads the want ads in the jungle on the banks of the South Platte River, Denver skyline in background.

Don in the hotel room we rented for him, Denver. Pictures of his kids in foreground.

The Denver skyline—shiny and young and alive, in contrast to some Rust Bowl cities—shrinks behind us, and we are back on the plains, gliding along in the dubious comfort of the bus. Before long, the cramped seats make us wish we were on an eastbound freight instead. But a train would be too slow. We must hurry back to St. Louis, where our car awaits our return in a parking lot. There are more things to be seen, more roads to be covered in the middle part of the country.

A farm woman from Colby, Kansas, and her sister occupy the seat in front of ours. Things aren't good these days for people of the land, either, the farm woman says. Between interest rates and crop prices, cattlemen and wheat farmers can't earn enough to make it worth their while, she says. Drought threatens, too, with the water table under Kansas drying up. She and her husband will do okay, no matter, she adds. They own their land free and clear, and if times get bad enough, she says they'll be able to raise enough truck crops to feed themselves.

Colby comes, and they leave. It is dark when the bus resumes its journey. We peer out the window, wondering what will happen to Don. We've got maybe a buck and four bits left between us, having bought our $72 tickets with plastic money. No self-respecting hobo should leave home without Mastercard. We spent two hundred greenbacks to get Don a room in a cheap hotel, which drained our wallets. We couldn't leave him on the streets. We worried he wouldn't make it. With a room for one month, maybe he'll be able to find work. But what of the hundreds of other Dons walking around Denver? We were powerless to help them. So we helped one. Big deal. It doesn't seem fair.

We don't sleep, don't speak during the twenty-four or so hours it takes to traverse the dull miles across Kansas and Missouri. In St. Louis we hastily fix a flat and continue our search, racing with deliberate speed nonstop into the South, into the void.

Don shaves before going to seek work.

Hopping "on the fly," a dangerous practice. David is at a critical point here. If his foot misses that lower bar, it will glide under the wheels, "giant salami-slicers," as one old-time hobo calls them. Colton rail yard, east of Los Angeles.

Hoboes get off a southbound, Western Pacific yard, Sacramento, while our group waits for a northbound.

The end of a ride.

Couple waiting to ride north,
Oroville, California.

Ron, who once built nuclear power plants, caught a freight train into the Denver hobo jungle. He eats a tomato harvested from a dumpster, cooked in a stew simmered in an old tackle box.

A rail rider waves to other hoboes from his perch on a "pig" rolling south through California's Central Valley.

Shack in Denver, Rio Grande & Western rail yard, Salt Lake City.

Hoboes waiting for a train,
Denver skyline in background.

85

86

Ken, an unemployed construction worker with four children, waits for a train in Salt Lake City so he can embark on a job hunt. This is the first time he has tried to ride a freight train.

Ken sleeps on a pig as the train lumbers up the Colorado River canyon east of Grand Junction, Colorado.

There is little romance to riding the rails when the train Ken is on enters the seven-mile-long Moffat Tunnel on top of the Continental Divide. The men choke on diesel smoke.

As the train descends the Front Range of the Rockies into Denver, it gets cold. Ken huddles in his sleeping bag.

Before going to look for work, Ken washes in the South Platte River the day after the train pulled in the yard.

Ken nervously enters a trailer at a construction site in Denver to see if they need any laborers.

He is told no, and he exits, dejected.
He rode out on the next freight to Texas.

Busted by two bulls, this hobo in the Southern Pacific rail yard in Yuma, Arizona, is thrown off a train about to pull out for California.

Dusk, train moving out, Texas.

Erik and Alvena.

Chapter 6: "BROKE DOWN"

The highway leads into the hills of Tennessee, past thick hardwood forests, tumbledown barns sporting faded chewing tobacco ads, tired fields of red earth waiting to be plowed. We leave the open road and turn onto the streets of Chattanooga, a Tennessee River town near the Georgia border reminiscent of southern cities of the 1950s and early 1960s. Buildings, not too tall, nor too glassy, are properly aged; the people terribly polite, but not very friendly. Change seems banished to a permanent vacation.

We drive to the Interstate 24 on and off ramps, to see who's hitchhiking through. At the first ramp we come to, a gray-haired man and woman thrust their thumbs skyward as if holding imaginary torches in imitation of the Statue of Liberty. Their clothes are wrinkled and fatigued, like their faces.

Her eyes are simply cadaverous. Never before have we seen eyes like those, so full of hunger, worry, desperation. She is not more than fifty, but they age her another three decades. His eyes beg the passing cars, following each like a dog watching a T-bone steak being passed at a dinner table.

Erik is his name, hers Alvena. Two hours of standing here, and no ride, says Erik, an unemployed metalworker.

They sold their car to make their last rent payment on their Louisville apartment to forestall eviction that came anyway. That's why they're thumbing, he says, searching for work.

Alvena sits on one of their suitcases, wrapped in her heavy coat, hands crossed on her lap as if in prayer. She does not offer much conversation, and looks down at the ground, reading it like a book. It is hard not to stare at her eyes. Erik notices this. He takes us aside. We don't have to ask: he tells us he has to get her off the streets soon, but doesn't know how. His eyes dart and he whispers excitedly. What do I do, goddammit! What do I do! Our mouths fall open dumbly and we have no advice. What does he do? I run to the car and procure bread and jelly for lunch sandwiches. Alvena downs hers as if swallowing a glass of water. Last night, she says, the owner of a diner let them eat for free.

He tells us about a man named Ed, whom they met at the Salvation Army last night. Ed, says Erik, is a sheet metal worker from Kentucky, out of work for many months. He began traveling with his three children in search of work, but his car died when he got to Chattanooga three days ago.

"Had no place to stay last night," says Erik. "Went to the Sally. Full up. Ed comes out. Says we can sleep in his car. It was better than sleeping under a bridge. You gotta talk to him. He's got no money. He's in a hell of a mess. We're all in a hell of a mess."

As we approach, Ed's son, maybe twelve years old, tries to dribble a flat basketball in the parking lot of the Salvation Army, next to his dad's broken-down sedan. The ball goes thunk, thunk, thunk, sticking to the ground like a big gob of peanut butter with each futile bounce.

The boy runs to get Dad.

Ed comes out. He's a giant man, with short-cropped red hair—and those hands! They seem big enough to hold a football like a hard-boiled egg. It seems he was once strong, very macho, but that was some other time, some other place.

His eyes are cemented on the lawn as his feet scrape through the grass. His face is paralyzed, vacant, the color of yellow squash, wearing the kind of expression you find among victims of an avalanche, earthquake, or fire.

We ask what he's going to do, where he's going to look for work.

"Look, buddy, I don't know what I'm going to do," he says hoarsely. His eyes remain fixed on the ground, never looking at us. "Buddy, I don't know where I'm going. Buddy . . . I . . . don't want to talk anymore . . ."

He slumps on the lawn and hides his face, crying softly. We retreat in a quick backstep. The son watches with an owlish look, continuing to bounce the ball.

Thunk. Thunk. Thunk.

Hitchhiker on the way to Texas has given up and sleeps at the side of the road.

Chapter 7: **GHOST CITY**

Michigan blacks. Pennsylvania yellows. Ohio whites. Seen through the blurry windshield, the parade of license plates passes. Late-model specials, clinking along on hope and luck, laden with suitcases, sleeping bags, clothes.

Some are tourists or visitors here on business, for sure. Gentlemen travelers trekking down this rainy highway for unfathomable reasons, in tidy autos with suits and dresses on hangers blocking the rear windows. HoJo hoboes—the Howard Johnson set.

They are easy to differentiate from the buckless vagabonds bound for Birmingham and beyond.

The rubbertramps have familiar despairing faces, the kind of mugs we saw in Youngstown. Their backs are twisted to the shape of car seats, it seems, from sleeping so many nights in their four-wheeled hard-times hotels. The back seats are mobile jungles, piled with soda pop cans, hamburger wrappers, and soiled blankets.

They start appearing outside Chattanooga. Three middle-aged men in a station wagon from Pennsylvania are first, coming fast up the left lane. The one occupying the passenger seat reads a map.

His face says, Gawd, get us there, let's find some work.

A young couple from Michigan are next. They have been at this for some time, as the car looks as if it's been their home for weeks.

Her face says, Gawd, get us home, we ain't gonna find work.

Miles later, we pass a lone man, unshaven for days, lurching along in the right lane in a van listing like a sinking ship. The shocks on the passenger side are busted.

His face says, Gawd, I've been out for months, I don't know where I'm going and there ain't no home to go back to.

What are their stories? The impersonality of the superhighway makes it impossible to learn.

Darkness finds us near Birmingham. Soon, we are in the middle of a pine forest, on a two-lane mountain road barely visible through the rain-blasted windshield. It's a perfect set for a cheap horror movie, the scene just before the ghouls attack. You always wonder why the murdered fools ever ventured to such a place. We pull to the edge of the roadside ditch and sleep.

The radio blares commercials. The dull announcer pitches a deal you *can't* miss at some furniture store. Listen to Birmingham's *best* rock. Drink at *this* bar, and meet the cool set.

Idle men, Employment Security Division, Little Rock, Arkansas.

Billboards assault the eyes. Ride this motorcycle, and you're a real man. Drink this whiskey, and women will be all over you. Come to Marlboro country. Buy! Buy! Buy! You notice how much money we're encouraged to spend when you're going to find those men and women who can't buy.

We pull off the interstate and begin the routine, practiced in each city through which we pass. First, we head for the rail yard. Ninety percent of the time you'll find the blood bank, missions, and hangout park nearby. It is at these places we're most likely to find the new poor.

Once, in a city we'd never before visited, we bet each other that within five minutes, we could find the mission, jungle, and blood bank, without a map, without asking anyone. It took precisely four minutes. It was a depressing bet to win.

Birmingham is no exception.

A few blocks from the yard, at the Jimmie Hale Rescue Mission, men lie sleeping under the eaves on the sidewalk, scattered human cordwood. We stand back, assessing the situation.

A woman drives up in a brand-new Oldsmobile, rolls down the window, and with a grimace thrusts her hand into the rain. It's loaded with a fistful of dollar bills. A group of men awaken and pluck them. She fishtails off as fast as the car will take her.

Many are drunk homeguards and look as if they've been on the streets for years, though you never know. It doesn't take long to degenerate. All the same, we choose not to wade through them.

In the yard, old boxcars boasting romantic names of dead railroads swallowed up in corporate mergers or simply allowed to die, fill the siding tracks like an army of giant steel ants: Penn Central. Rock Island. Frisco.

Local toughs wearing watch caps hang out, shifting back and forth from foot to foot, eyeing us from behind the cover of wraparound sunglasses, looking as mean as they probably are. The best defense is to appear more vicious than potential opponents. We twirl clubs carried for that purpose. Up the tracks, next to a dead steel mill, we find the jungle, under a darkened, elevated bridge at least a mile long, with dozens of support pillars that seem to march infinitely to the east. We imagine a gunman behind each. To the south, an Illinois Central halts on the main line, but doesn't drop its air. A staggering drunk homeguard tries to cross over a knuckle, but can't lift himself, so he creeps beneath the wheels. We're too far away to stop him. The train could snap at any second, slicing him in half.

Come night, a number of blocks away, men climb the stairs of the Salvation Army. They have big packs, heavy feet, and desire sleep, not talk. We let them be.

This Sally shines. Newcomers are checked in at a tiny office.

"We're gearing up for a worsening situation," says Major Ralph Morrel. "There will be a lot of people on the road for a long time. People think the steel mills will reopen, the coal mines will reopen. They're not going to open again. These folks are in trouble. The more people we see, the more desperate they are."

Back on the street, the car carries us on our way.

"People's moving," Mark tells us as he looks off at the setting sun framed by the open door of a mission further west. "Once you lose your home, there ain't nothin' worth stayin' for. I'm afraid. But I'm more afraid of staying back there. It's better to leave. I'd rather have a chance of gettin' work and making a little bit less. When you hit that road, you feel you're part of something. After that first hunnert miles, you know you're doing the right thing."

Mark, flanked by his two teenage sons in football jerseys,

seems at peace with being on the road, but an uneasiness in his voice tells us he's scared.

We spend maybe a half hour with Mark and his sons—watching the orange sun stalk into night—jabbering about politics and life. Most days, we meet people like them. We hear their stories. We extend wishes of good luck. We move on. We never really get to know most of them; such is life on the road. They are friends of the hour. Surprisingly, many insist on telling complete strangers their problems, a thing they might never have done in good times. And if you get a man on the tramp around a campfire, he will often reveal secrets dating to the time he came from the womb. It seems to be therapy, a way of absolving the devilish worries in your soul, and ah, what the hell! You'll never see each other again.

So it is with Mark.

Their car blew up west of Birmingham, he tells us. In a gas station, where the car was towed, they met three other job-seeking men, traveling just like them. Mark says they hitched a ride with the men and continued their westward journey, toward Los Angeles. This is the second forced move for the divorced father and his sons. Almost two years ago, he says they left Grand Rapids, Michigan, for a better life in Atlanta—until he was again laid off from his job as a printer.

"Things go slowly," says Mark. "You lose the TV. And you accept that. You lose the car. And you accept that. Then you cut down on the groceries. And you accept that. Then you lose the house. That's too much. It's like a cancer. It eats you up. You gotta fight back. The hardest part is leaving. After you leave, though, it's okay."

A conflagration of thick green brush along the banks of the Arkansas River in Little Rock seems as if it could almost conceal the Red Army. Spring has finally arrived, at least here in the South.

We are finally entering serious hobo country. We've found the number of rail riders increases as one heads west. Maybe it's the open country, warmer climates, or that people only ride freights once they're far from home and utterly broken down. Signs of minijungles abound—scorch marks from recent fires etched on bridge pillars; hollowed-out lairs under bushes where men nested on sheets of cardboard for a night.

The big camps, however, the ones we were told about by Dennis Hamilton, head of the Union Rescue Mission, are elusive. These jungles, used in the 1930s, have seen a revival, Hamilton told us back at the mission. The mission was built with the labor of hoboes from the same era.

"It's like the thirties. They hear about us through word of mouth. Word gets around. Men know they need to listen. So they become good listeners," Hamilton said. "In Houston, if they don't find work, they go on to California. Or they double back. There may be seven guys in one car. They team up to go from place to place."

We feel a strange sense of the past here. Mopacs bawl out of the yard on the main line. If steam whistled out of the units, it would be easy to believe we've been jettisoned back to 1933.

We continue looking for the camps, which have names like Camp One or Sugar Shack. In one tangle of shrubs, we find Dan, scrunched inside a dwarf shed made of clear sheet plastic. He pokes his head out like a nervous woodchuck. It's hard to tell if he's been shy all his life, or if the streets have made him an introvert.

Two years ago, he tells us, he left Chicago on a job hunt through Texas and California. He failed, so he came here. Now, he lives in this lean-to, hard-scrabbling for survival. He sells blood plasma, collects aluminum cans that he sells for scrap, and harvests food from dumpsters. Dozens of onions and tomatoes taken from a grocery store's trash bin testify to his eating habits, littering the ground around his feet. He points to the location of Camp One through the forest.

Dan. Dumpster vegetables to his left will be his dinner.

Ghost village.

"There were a bunch of people there . . . families and stuff," he says. "But they all caught a freight to Texas a few days ago."

Even with directions, the camp is hard to find. It appears suddenly, a little village of a half-dozen cardboard and plastic huts flanking a tiny creek. These folks were secretive. They took great care to build their town where it wouldn't be seen, not wanting to parade their poverty. Yet they were very near the world of wealth: The dome of the Arkansas state capitol is visible through the trees.

The shantytown looks "live," and we approach with caution. A man's camp is his house. You do not trespass without asking permission.

A holler of "hello in camp" brings no response, so it seems safe to enter.

It's obvious many people called this encampment home for some months. Neatly arranged rows of silverware are ready for the next meal that was never cooked. Pots and pans hang from poles and in trees. Little chairs surround the fire pit. A bra hanging from a tree limb tells of a petite woman; a toy truck and scattered diapers inform us she had a small child.

The huts are well made—nailed together and properly footed in the ground. Womanly touches abound. The inside of the shacks are well manicured. Some contain beds on raised platforms. Next to one bed is a Bible, a Western novel, a can of unopened snuff.

These folks hastily abandoned the premises, leaving behind anything too heavy to carry. Who were they? Where did they come from? What made them have to live like this? If only the orphaned household goods could talk. The artifacts raise more questions than they answer.

A Mopac rumbles by, unseen through the forest, but close enough to shake the earth. Heading west, to Texas. We follow.

Silverware, neatly arranged for a meal never cooked, abandoned in ghost village.

More idle men, Open Door Mission, Houston.

Chapter 8: **YANKEES IN THE PROMISED LAND**

For six blocks, police tail our car through the downtown area. Finally, the cop flashes his rooftop lights, pulling us over. One of Houston's finest sashays forward, hand on gun.

He eyes the Ohio license plates, the hardhat in the rear window, the Youngstown State University decal. He doesn't know, but he speaks into a tape recorder hidden on the front seat.

"How long you been here?" he demands.

Two days.

"We know. We saw this car when you came in. Watcha doing here?"

We waffle, never really answering the question.

"Well, how long you staying?"

About another week.

"Okay. If we see this car here past one more week, I'm going to throw you in jail!"

We ask, What for?

The cop puts his hand on his chin and squints, examining the car for an excuse. After a minute, he points to the worn wheels. "Tires!"

Our crime? Having Ohio plates and being suspected of coming here to look for work.

While driving on the interstate a few days later, a pickup truck sporting a "Native Texan" bumper sticker throttles around us. Its driver spits. A huge, hideous hocker twirls with unbelievable accuracy through the air and splats against the windshield. The driver and his two passengers laugh heartily.

Then, when parked on a street, a man pulls up, looks at the Ohio plate, and screams, "Asshole!"

Welcome to Texas, pardner.

"Yankees are like hemorrhoids. If they come down and go back, that's all right. But if they come down and stay, they can be a constant source of irritation." —B. K. Johnson, onetime chief of the Houston Police Department. At the time of our visit, Johnson is an assistant chief to the force of thirty-four hundred officers.

Youngstown people who'd unsuccessfully come here looking for work told endless tales of harassment. One said the police stopped him in downtown Houston. When they heard he was job-hunting, they escorted him to the freeway and told him never to return to this city of two million, the fifth largest in the nation. From the descriptions given by the Youngstowners, the police who stopped us followed a routine script: (1) Find out why you're here. (2) If the answer is to look for work, there is just and probable cause to hassle you.

Our welcome by the Houston Police is not an isolated

Houston is mean.

incident, admits Houston police spokeswoman Phymeon Jackson: "Yes, there have been complaints. Especially from Michigan people. There's an anti-northern bias."

Police can be your least worry. Some northern industrial refugees complained to Houston authorities they were chased off by shotgun-wielding vigilantes.

For a time, some of the jobless found a safe home in Tent City, the celebrated camp on the banks of the San Jacinto River that captured international attention in 1982. Tent City became more of a circus than a real home when it was overpublicized. But it symbolized the plight of the unemployed in the Sunbelt.

It was then closed and bulldozed, ostensibly because of a fire death there. But the real reason, many Yankees suspect, was that the impromptu town gave Houston a bad name.

That suspicion is fueled by statements such as those made to the *Wall Street Journal* by Texas State Representative Ed Emmett. Tent City was being "orchestrated" by the "Eastern media. They want to keep the publicity flowing to damage our reputation," he told the *Journal*.

In retaliation, the Republican legislator from Houston sponsored a successful bill making it a crime to sleep under bridges, and for anyone but "overnight" campers to stay in roadside parks. He'd learned those things were not illegal under Texas law.

At one time, Texans advertised for people to come live in their state. That's when unemployment was in low single-digit figures. At the peak of migration, officials estimate fifteen hundred people a week were coming to Houston. When 10 percent unemployment found its way here, however, they began despising anyone who would come and "take" their jobs.

Texans rage at programs like one in Ohio that paid unemployed workers to come to the Lone Star State. The Ohio River steel- and shoe-manufacturing center of Portsmouth decided rather than let some residents starve, it was better to use almost a half million dollars in federal grants to relocate them to Longview, Texas, and attempt to get them jobs there.

"We're tired of people from the North," says one woman. "They're taking our jobs. We feel like they're invading our country."

As one Northerner observes: "If you're here on vacation, you're a Yankee. If you're looking for work, you're a damn Yankee. If you find work, you're a fucking damn Yankee."

Some Texans, however, are not alone in their hatred for the new poor.

Los Angeles made it illegal to sleep in cars. In Fort Lauderdale, a city commissioner suggested spraying garbage with kerosene or insecticide to discourage foraging—to get rid of vermin, he said, you cut the food supply. Phoenix systematically forced missions to close.

No place seems to want the new homeless.

Houston is a mirage.

To a casual visitor with a fat wallet driving into downtown off Interstate 45, it is an impressive city. Skyscrapers covered with acres of glass and steel dot the horizon; the lush expanse of Sam Houston Park beckons; the streets are spacious, clean; men and women in smart clothes bustle between office buildings; it's clearly a city on the move, a major force in the New South.

But beneath this veneer lies another world. To see it, you must drive beyond the glitter of glass and plastic.

Start by going behind the skyscrapers, over to the Star Hope Rescue Mission on La Branch. There, hundreds of men sit on street curbs—their faces buried in their hands—idle, like so many discarded, broken gears scattered and rusting at a shuttered steel mill.

Hang around for a while. Watch the timeless world of

An old woman with a cup begs for nickels.

Men sitting idle outside the Star Hope Rescue Mission.

these men. Watch a man spend a full five minutes rolling a cigarette, savoring each moment, because it may be the most exciting thing that will happen in his day.

Watch police cruise slowly past. Watch the cops return and glare, convicting you with their eyes. Suddenly, you feel like a murderer. Breathe a sigh of relief when they move on, only to stop and arbitrarily question two other men. Watch, if you can, when the cops beat their heads bloody with nightsticks for no reason, then haul the two off to jail.

Watch men mob the front door when the mission opens. Two hundred is the limit. When it's reached, the rest are turned away, condemned to spend the night on the streets. Watch a mother and father come begging for help with their son. Dad is dressed in old U.S. Marine clothes. Mom holds her forehead to assuage a headache, towing the toddling boy, barely old enough to walk. Watch them slink off, Dad gritting his teeth and venting his anger at the boy. The mission cannot help them. Families in search of emergency lodging are plain out of luck; at the time of our visit, there's no place for them to stay in Houston.

Leave the mission area and drive around. Notice the outcasts scavaging for recyclable cans and food in dumpsters; find them huddled in abandoned, charred buildings that smell of piss and rot; on a sidewalk, look at the crouched, wrinkled woman, cup in her outstretched hands as she begs for nickels; go to the blood bank, where dozens of people stand hours in line for the privilege of selling their blood for as little as $7.00.

Get out of your car. Walk in the little valley formed by Buffalo Bayou, a river looping around downtown; its waters reflect the images of those beautiful million-dollar skyscrapers.

They mirror another scene—the hungry faces of hopeless men as they wash in the swarthy liquid. They live here, in this place some call Bayou Alley.

Cross under the Smith Street Bridge. You'll find two of these residents, both named Jim, camped here in clear violation of the law sponsored by Mr. Emmett. They're cooking dinner. Come into their home.

A fire crackles deep in the recesses of Hole-in-the-Wall, the name they've given to the underside of this bridge. It's a fitting title for the forbidding grotto facing the still waters of the bayou. This is their kitchen, they explain. Their bedroom is upriver, also under a bridge, a place they call the "apartment."

The apartment is just one of many camps under the bridges. They have given names to those places, too: the Grand Canyon (for its deep gullies), Green Acres (it's verdant), Fort Stockton (it's safe from attack). Those camps are full of others just like them.

Old Jim has been on the road for ten years. He is new Jim's mentor, teaching him the world of the streets.

New Jim came to Houston one month ago on a bus from Akron, Ohio. In Akron, he was living with a relative, on welfare, and hated it. Before hard times forced him on the dole, he was a bouncer in a Cleveland bar; before that, a roadie for a band; before that, a worker at a ski resort. Sure, he screwed off in the past, he says, jumping from job to job, not really caring. But there was always some other job to go to. All of a sudden, there isn't.

New Jim is a laborer, not a Socratic thinker. A big man, he likes using his back. He enjoys work. He enjoys drinking beer after the work is done. And he enjoys women. He is quiet behind his bearded face.

At first, he stayed at the Star Hope. Right away, he found work in a day-labor pool, and later, at the Houston Astrodome. His job at the Astrodome is only four hours a day, two or three days a week. He doesn't earn enough to pay rent on a real apartment.

"I hope to be able to get a place soon. I never did this before. The worst I ever had it was when I had to sleep in my car a couple of days when I was going to school. I've gotten used to the bats," he says, eyeing hordes of swooping

New Jim and old Jim wake up in their "apartment" under a bridge.

winged creatures that have sallied forth to greet the first darkness of evening. Their pitched squeals form an eerie whine. He shivers. "But I can't stand the rats!"

As he speaks, a rat, illuminated by firelight, clambers over the roof of a hut built at the rear of Hole-in-the-Wall. The rodent's eyes are red coals. Overhead, each passing car hits a manhole cover with a loud clunk!

New Jim explains he doesn't need an alarm to wake for work—morning rush-hour traffic shakes the roof of the apartment enough to arouse him.

We walk down to the bank of the bayou and watch dark water swirl at our feet. From down here, the buildings are invisible, and it's easy to imagine we're back in frontier times, when the world was ruled by the club, the gun, the knife. Up the hill, old Jim feeds the fire. His shadow is twelve feet tall on the walls of the cavern. A voice comes from the obscure shadow that is new Jim's face.

"Maybe they gotta start a war. Maybe that'll get people working again."

Joe Marshall, Sr., said the same thing back in Youngstown, and we'd heard such comments in various missions. People say it half in jest, but there's a serious edge to the voices.

We climb the dusty slope back to the fire, and fix sandwiches made from canned stew spread on bread. Old Jim picks up his sandwich, but drops it, drawing his foot-long knife. He peels into the darkness, screaming, "C'mon, motherfuckers! C'mon!"

Two machete-wielding men had sneaked through the shadows to within twenty feet of the camp. New Jim grabs a club from the woodpile and readies for battle. The invaders, not far ahead of old Jim, crash off through the brush, and all is safe.

"I don't want to keep living like this," he sighs, while awaiting old Jim's return. "I can't bring girls down here."

New Jim and old Jim next to their fire.

Jim, Bonnie, kids, in the big tent.

Chapter 9: **HOME SWEET TENT**

A sluggard dragon's breath of a wind wafts across the swamp—a buggy, brushy home to cottonmouths, fire ants, and other unspeakable creatures. It is a time of misery, these hot torpid Texas afternoons. Even the warlike fire ants, whose bite feels like the burn of an electric shock, are slothful even when prodded with a stick as they lounge outside their dens.

Across the field of grass burnt brown by the flamethrower sun, the walls of three canvas cottages flap in the breeze. The tents are clustered around a platform made of scrap lumber, built in haste to raise the "living room" (the area between the tents under a sun awning) above winter flood-waters that poured from the marsh. The water, full of vociferous frogs, has receded, but still laps just behind eleven-year-old Matthew's "bedroom," the smallest of the tents. A Houston *Post*, folded to the help-wanted section, rests next to the television. Zinnias planted around the perimeter look almost suburban.

Bonnie has just finished tidying twelve-year-old Jennifer's bedroom. She zips the door closed and reaches into the near-empty cooler to make a supper of sandwiches. Jim sits in a rusting glider couch—covered with cankered, bleached cushions—rocking back and forth, scanning the swamp. Sweat rains off his forehead. His mouth beneath his mus-tache is downturned. He quit a job in disgust today and is wondering if he did the right thing. Bonnie, with a mouth that looks like it laughs a lot, is smiling. Things haven't been going well lately for the Alexander family, for sure, but Jennifer and Matthew's latest grade-school report cards were salted with A's. And above all else, the kids are what count.

Jim worked in a Michigan salt mine, we would later learn when we got drunk and he was laughing and screaming and throwing beer cans across a pool hall. We end up spending one week with the family, sleeping in our car near them in a campground north of Houston.

They began living here a month ago after Jim was laid off from a well-paying job as a welder in the oil fields. They could no longer afford their $500 apartment. It is only the latest thing to happen to them since they came to Texas. Their odyssey began four years ago, when their home was foreclosed by the bank in Port Huron, Michigan, after Jim lost his job in the salt mine and couldn't find other work.

The sunset blazes, setting the swamp aglow. The air is an invisible sponge, moist with a haze that hangs thick and fierce and low. The cloud of superheated fog extinguishes the sun long before it reaches the horizon. A wolf pack of mosquitoes rises from the marsh and marches upon the world.

Bonnie shows us around their home. She and Jim live in the big tent, bought with money earned from selling their washer and dryer when they left their apartment. It contains a double bed and nightstand. She apologizes for the unkempt appearance—yesterday, a spring windstorm wreaked havoc. Jennifer and Matthew play with the dogs, Bear and Boo. The dogs bark and the kids bellow. Bonnie slaps at the mosquitoes.

Bonnie introduces us to Cindi and John, neighbors living in the adjoining tent site of this commercial campground. Cindi and John, from Cincinnati, Ohio, say they, too, moved here because they couldn't afford to keep their apartment. To help defray camping fees, Bonnie works in the campground office. There are few, if any, legal free places to camp around Houston since the closure of Tent City.

Cindi shows off a sink John made for her. "This is great," she says. "I never want to live in a house again. Look, we got fresh air. No hassles. I'm sorry we didn't start living like this years ago."

Right. John nods. Jim and Bonnie's heads bob up and down, too, and their words reflect agreement.

Their voices ring hollow. Pride is the genesis of many lies. There is more truth to be learned here. We take Jim out for a night of playing pool.

Jim sticks his tongue out and takes aim down the stick. He fires. The cue ball careens and scratches in the corner pocket. "Well, it's been a long time," he says.

We crack Lone Star beers, offering him one. No thanks, says Jim, gave it up two years ago, just drink coffee now. It makes me feel my Wheaties, gets me in too many fights, and Bonnie doesn't like me coming home drunk, he says. He wins the first game. Oh, what the hell, it's hot, he says, just one beer. Another game. Well, just one more, he says. Another game. Another beer. and so on into the night.

He was wild years ago, he tells us. 'Specially after he came home from 'Nam, he drawls through lips deadened from too many Lone Stars. He was a U.S. Marine during the Tet Offensive, and damn proud of it, he says. He came home, married Bonnie, bought a three-bedroom home, and started to settle down. One day, he tells us, he walked into what he thought was a meeting of the National Rifle Association but was instead a gathering of the American Independent Party. He turned to leave, but they invited him to stay. One hour later, he walked out a candidate for the Michigan State Assembly. He lost, but he says he was proud he could run

Jim sinks an eight ball. He whoops. It must be the fifteenth game. When he puts his quarters in the slots, he discovers the little door to the money inside is broken and easily pops open. He withdraws fistfuls of coins. "What the hell . . . they make enough money off it. You gotta get a break once in a while," he says. We play for free the rest of the night. He racks the balls and pitches another empty beer can at the wall.

He didn't want to bring his family to live in a tent, he tells us. That was failure. But he had no choice when they were kicked out of their apartment. The job he started a few weeks ago paid the federal minimum, $3.35 an hour. His paycheck was enough to pay for food and gas, but not the rent. "I lived in tents in Vietnam. I went through a typhoon in one," he says. He falls quiet for a moment. The windstorm of the other day brought back a lot of those memories.

Vietnam is very much alive in his mind, an experience he is still sorting out, one he may never understand.

"I joined the Marines when I was seventeen. I'd go on patrol, walking through the jungle. Once, I was standing in

Jennifer, Matthew, dogs Bear and Boo, and two puppies.

The family and their neighbors.

a clump of trees, and a 'gook' walked by me, about eight feet away. You want to know what scared is? I froze. I was afraid he could hear the sweat dripping off my nose. I really thought he could hear it. Things like that mess you up. I came out thinking I was tough. I was a Marine! I'd walk into bars and open my big mouth and get into fights. I don't think I ever won any. I'd pick the biggest guys. I was just feelin' my Wheaties."

He's begun to lose badly at pool, but he isn't thinking about the game anymore. He quit his minimum-wage job in a welding shop, he says, because he was ridiculed by fellow workers, Texans who hate Northerners. He says he's glad he walked out, but his voice reveals he's not sure. The price of wounded pride may mean his family doesn't eat. It must have been intolerable at that job, because it's obvious he has a lot of love for his family.

"I earned in one week what I used to earn in one day at that job. Talk about exploitation. I kept getting called a dumb Yank and made fun of. You're not accepted. I couldn't take it anymore. The good ol' boys let the dummies from the North do all the work.

"I've been in a foreign country where the signs say 'Yankee, go home.' And you get called a Yankee down here! It's a culture shock. For the first time in my life, I know what it's like to be on the receiving end of prejudice. I tell these Texans they should go to a foreign country and feel what it's like to be called a Yankee. I feel like an invader from the North. I feel like a foreigner in my own country. If the opportunities don't exist where you're from, where do you play ball?

"I'll tell you what's happened to us. I rolled a few stop signs near Galena Park. I went to jail for twenty-four hours because of it. The cops wouldn't even let me make a call. Bonnie was worried sick. I didn't get smart with them, because I'd heard the stories. If you're a Yankee, don't go to jail down here. They're meaner than cat shit."

It's time to go home.

Jim replaces a respectable number of quarters in the slot, and we stagger with him back to his tent through the early morning darkness. The air is alive, and so are we. We holler. A dog barks. Jim tells wonderful stories about wonderful women he knew years ago. He sobers up enough near the tent to worry that Bonnie might be angry he broke his vow of abstaining from booze. He shushes Bear and Boo, slipping in through the door, trying not to awaken her. Muffled whispers tell us he isn't quiet enough. Though we cannot discern the conversation, Bonnie's words sound kind.

It is our last night with the family. We offer to make dinner for them and their neighbors before we move on to Mexico. We buy shopping bags full of food, fixings for slumgullion stew—a hearty mix of ground meat, noodles, and whatever else you can fit into the pot—everything including the proverbial kitchen sink, though in this case, that means everything including the contents of the Coleman cooler. The children excitedly run to the stove to inspect the progress of the meal. Jennifer, who will be a beautiful woman someday, peers in the pot. "We don't have to eat bologna sandwiches tonight!" she announces with glee.

The stew, simmered in the biggest kettle, is soon reduced to a few bottom scrapings. Matthew and Jennifer return three times for extra helpings. Jim wrestles with Matthew for a while, and the kids run off and play a game, quibbling as only siblings can. He puts his arm around his wife of thirteen years, sucks on a Marlboro, then stokes the fire to ward off the dampness of evening. Tonight, he drinks coffee.

A wind blows across the swamp. The air is beset with the gossip of night birds. In the distance, a Southern Pacific freight rumbles through the night, its diesel horns blaring. The urban call of the wild. It seems everywhere we go, the unemployed always wind up near the tracks, even if they don't ride the rails.

Bonnie gets up and chases the kids to bed. Like most kids, they whine, wanting to stay awake with the adults. As they dress in pajamas, the forms of their bodies perform a shadow dance inside the brightly lit tents glowing like blue and orange Chinese lanterns.

With the children gone, Jim leans forward and begins talking about things he didn't want to say when they were around. His face takes on an electric, supernatural glow in the pale firelight.

"Material possessions are meaning less and less to me. The way the whole economy is going, it's a good time to be highly mobile," says Jim. "There's an undercurrent in this country. An undercurrent people in power are not aware of. They don't realize the bitterness and anger they are stirring

up. There's a bitterness seething that will erupt. There's going to be rioting in the streets."

He talks collectively, but it seems a mask for his own frustrations, his inability to deal with a problem so utterly out of his control.

Jim chucks a butt into the flames, clamps another cigarette in his lips, flicking his lighter with an anger that makes the flame leap wildly.

"I'm not a philosopher. But when the middle class erupts, they're going to be sorry. Uncle Sugar hasn't learned that better-educated people will be out to change something that is their right to change. I never thought this would happen to me. I never thought this could happen in America. I've gone from the land of plenty to nothing. And we're living in the lap of luxury compared to a lot of people."

Jim crawls in the master tent and procures a .357 Magnum revolver he wants to show us. One of his proudest possessions, it shines in the firelight. His long arm makes a sweeping arc, motioning to the empty swamps and fields around him—all of it privately owned land.

"They won't let you use that land to survive. I could go out there and grow a lot of food. If you try that, they'll arrest you and put you in jail. This is America! There was a time when all we had to eat was one potato between all four of us."

"Boy, I sliced it real thin," says Bonnie.

"The kids went to bed *hungry* that night," Jim adds. The word "hungry" rolls out of his throat like a grunt made as if someone is jabbing a fist in his gut. He clutches the gun in his shaking hand. "I'm *never* going to let that happen again. I'm trying my damnedest as an upright citizen. First, I'll go hunting for food. If that doesn't work, I hit a 7-eleven. I'll hold up a store. I won't take money. But I'll take food. My kids won't starve."

Jim loads one of his guns.

These unemployed people hitched down from Michigan and hated Texas. They have no jobs to return to, but have given up. San Antonio.

San Antonio. A homeless man
sleeps under stairs.

Near a mission, El Paso, Texas.

A fifty-six-year-old electrician, laid off and unable to find work. He sleeps under the bridge next to the Southern Pacific tracks, waiting for a train. El Paso.

Graffito under bridge next to the tracks, El Paso.

Chapter 10: DOWN AND OUT IN MEXICO

Dust squalls billow across the narrow street choked with a curb-to-curb horde of humanity: pretty women in colorful dresses, boys in tight T-shirts with transistor radios plastered to their ears, old men pushing carts full of bananas and melons. A barker rushes to each passerby. "Wanna taxi? Pussy?" he asks. Only four bucks, he begs.

From the darkened depths of a bar crammed with sweaty patrons, the steady, booming monotone from the beat of a drum pours out to the sidewalk. A sign over an eatery boasts of roasted *pollo* and cold *cerveza*—chicken and beer.

Inside the *pollo* house, a sanctuary from the confusion of the street, a hundred or so patrons sit at chipped tables beneath rusted, slow-moving ceiling fans that squeal like mice, failing to stir a breeze to cool the stifling quarters. In the center, tortillas are furiously rolled by a group of women half hidden by a forest of dead chickens hanging from the ceiling.

So this is Ciudad Juárez. This metropolis of 1.5 million—the fifth largest in Mexico—hugs the border shared with El Paso, a city in extreme western Texas.

El Paso is one of the most popular illegal entry points along the two-thousand-mile border. Each day, hundreds of Mexicans wade the Rio Grande that divides the two towns, seeking a better life in the promised land of Los Estados Unidos.

At the same time, American economic refugees are legally crossing the border to live in Mexico—though the tide is much smaller.

Americans are attracted because if you have to live on $30 a week in the United States, you starve. In Mexico, you get fat.

An armload of peaches, bananas, and oranges costs $1.60 in the open-air *mercado*. A 23-cent jar of instant coffee would run around $2.00 in the states. At the chicken house, a meal for two of roasted *pollo*, *cerveza*, fresh-squeezed orange juice, and *quesadilla* comes to just under $3.00.

Americans filter into the chicken house. They are not *turistas*. A ringer for Fred C. Dobbs, the character played by Humphrey Bogart in the movie *The Treasure of the Sierra Madre*, shuffles in with his hands in his pockets. In several scenes, Bogart, sporting a three-day growth of beard, walked around a Mexican town asking other U.S. citizens, "Hey, buddy. Can you spare a dime for a fellow American?"

The Bogart look-alike asks no such question. He scrapes past and sits in a corner, gloomily sipping *cerveza*, nibbling tortillas, and snapping at children who come to beg pesos from him.

Jim Dillon walks down Calle Lerdo, hands in his pockets. He's not as slovenly as the Bogart clone, perhaps because of his youthful blond locks, but his walk is haggard. He turns and enters the Juárez Hotel, passes the clerk speaking into the phone in galloping bursts of Spanish, and climbs the dim staircase.

His two-buck-a-night room is spacious, as clean and sparse as a family doctor's waiting room, with a private bath and maid service. The same overpriced American dollar— which has hampered American corporations' ability to sell goods on the world market—has made it cheap for men like Dillon to come live in a foreign country.

Dillon flops on the bed, resting his head on a pillow. He's exhausted and sunburned, he tells us, from working outside all day. And he says he's still recovering from a meeting between his head and a pool cue in a bar a few weeks ago. He parts his hair and exhibits a nasty crease, earned from a disgruntled player who felt Jim was winning too many pesos in a game of eight ball.

He came to Juárez two months ago, because he'd heard it was a cheap place to live, he says over the noise of honking and gear grinding coming from the street. His car broke down in San Angelo, Texas, a stop on his job hunt from the Midwest. He abandoned the car. "I couldn't find work at all. Zilch. So I came here."

The first few months in Mexico were rough, he says. He had to survive on $18 a week from an El Paso blood bank. The day-labor pool in El Paso, crowded with job seekers, would not even talk with him. Finally, he literally stormed the owner's office demanding—actually begging—for work. The owner hired him.

On frequent days when there's no work at the labor

Jim Dillon.

pool, he says he hustles a few dollars by walking from door to door with a stencil set, painting house numbers on curbs in El Paso.

"I walk up to a door and say I'm a student. It works, because I only charge two bucks. It adds up quick. If I was trying to make it in America on twenty hours of work a week, I'd starve. Here, I have a private bath. Good food. I get laid for four bucks. Movies for seventy-five cents. I'm going to see Paul Newman tonight. When people in the states are paying four dollars for a movie, I pay seventy-five cents. I'm able to live the kind of life I'm accustomed to. It's a real party."

We walk back out to the street. When it comes time to part ways, he seems sad. Well, life isn't that idyllic, he admits. Jim's voice trails off. He says in a low voice that he feels he's stationed on Mars, imprisoned in a world in which he does not belong.

He is lonely. He wishes he could afford to go home.

He checks his wallet, folding a hundred-peso note. He strolls down the alley to the movie house for ninety minutes of escape.

The oncoming parade starts as a roar, overpowering the normal clamor on the crowded streets of Juárez, scattering street urchins, old men, spectators.

On top of the lead bus, bullhorns crackle and buzz Spanish rhetoric, trumpeting antigovernment messages directed at politicians on both sides of the border.

We climb onto the roof of the slow-moving vehicle and sit next to the speakers for a better view. Behind, five thousand people swarm forward, waving red banners, nail-studded clubs, window-sized pictures of Marx, Lenin, and Che Guevara. One sign reads: In Mexico, There Isn't a Crisis . . . Just Pure Misery.

Cause for the commotion is the annual May Day march by the Comité de Defensa Popular—the Committee for the Popular Defense, or CDP.

A journalist who has covered Mexico for years says he's never seen so many show up for a Communist rally.

The turnout underscores the emergency facing Mexico. The crippled economy is the worst in fifty years. Those who work in Juárez make the equivalent of two to four American dollars a day. In a sixteen-month period, the peso fell to one sixth of its former value. Before devaluation, Mexicans earned the equivalent of eight dollars a day.

Many of Mexico's difficulties stem from overzealous oil-based expansion that led to an $83 billion foreign debt. It has had difficulty keeping up with payments since oil revenues fell off following the glut of crude on the world market. If the country were to default, it would spell big trouble not only for itself, but for American banks—and ultimately the American people.

Mexico's problems are our problems.

As the economy worsened, the number of Mexicans fleeing illegally to America increased dramatically. The flood is hard to measure, but arrests by the U.S. Border Patrol increased 40 percent between 1982 and 1983. In a one-year period, one million Mexican nationals were captured. The Border Patrol admits it nabs only a fraction of those trying to cross.

A large number of these immigrants ride the freights once they're in America. They journey as far north as the Canadian border.

Juárez itself is a destination for many displaced Mexicans who run from the interior. Many live in squatters' villages—hundreds of cardboard shanties in the desert outside of town. The Communists have a lot of support from these squatters, says one journalist who grew up in Juárez. In those squalid barrios, political slogans calling for a boycott of the upcoming election are painted on the shacks.

The leftists spread wall posters urging a boycott of the upcoming election.

The May Day throng stops at cobblestoned Municipal Plaza. Women shade their heads with the red flags they waved while marching. The crowd listens intently to orators who advise their countrymen not to vote, and espouse radical solutions to Mexico's troubles.

A man who marched in the parade dressed in puppet clothes says his costume represents a factory leader who "exploits and represses" workers. He adds the Communist Party wants workers not to labor "more than eight hours for the miserable sum of two dollars. We want a change of government."

A crowd gathers around the puppet man, wanting to hear questions posed by American journalists. A party leader runs into the middle of the group, ordering them not to speak to us. The leader tells us ordinary people aren't supposed to have their own opinions.

The people disperse and refuse to talk further.

The next morning, down at the Rio Grande, we find groups of working-class Mexican nationals coming to America by wading the muddy river, which flows swiftly through a man-made concrete channel.

"*Otra día* (another day)," sighs a man who walks out of the water and climbs the embankment to a fence, the legs of his pants dripping wet. He tells us in thick Spanish that he was caught by the Border Patrol the other day and is trying again.

"I don't want nothing with the 'say-day-pay' (CDP)," he adds. He feels they might be worse than the present government. A tall man follows. He says he is crossing because he has no way to feed his three children back home.

A man wearing a hat with a General Motors label says he's not happy with the present government, and something has to change. He is crossing the border not because he wants to, he explains, but because in one day in the U.S., he can earn as much as he would in one week in his homeland. He joins the crowd bunched up in front of a fence, waiting for a safe time to race into downtown El Paso.

These men are like a flock of hunted mule deer. If one bolts because he fears "La Migra" is coming, they all run. Twice, they flee after false alarms, but the third time, a green Border Patrol van does approach.

The van screeches to a halt in the center of a gravel strip of no-man's-land between the river and the town of El Paso. The door swings open and an agent jumps out.

"You can't stop them," the agent tells us while eyeing the Mexicans milling behind the safety of the fence. "It's like water in your hands . . . it falls through your fingers. You can hold a little bit back, but not much. That's how we are. Most fall through our fingers."

Says another agent: "How can you feel animosity toward people who are just trying to make a living to support their family? If it were me, I'd do the same thing."

May Day rally, Juárez.

Mexican nationals waiting to cross the border near Yuma, Arizona.

"Burros," men who charge to carry passengers across the Rio Grande. Juárez-El Paso, Texas.

A "burro" wading the Rio Grande who
did not want his picture taken.

Crossing the border over a railroad bridge, Juárez-El Paso.

Men bolt like hunted deer, on the border,
Juárez-El Paso.

Running into America, El Paso.

Caught. Yuma, Arizona.

Someone lost his shirt crossing the barbed wire.
Yuma, Arizona, border crossing.

Al and Betty.

Chapter 11: **GRANDPARENTS**

Another dust storm pushes clouds of sand against the parched, puckered mountains encircling El Paso. Grit sinks into the skin, burns the eyes, muddies the throat.

Al and Betty shield their faces from the sandpapering breeze as they throw their suitcases into the trunk of the car. Thanks for the lift, says Al in a slightly coarse, nasal voice that betrays he once lived in Boston. This is Mouse, he says, introducing his wife of twenty-six years by her nickname. They hug.

We speed west out of town, trading the ramshackle sprawl of El Paso for the sterility of the open desert, a world of sky, rock, smoke trees, and creosote bushes.

The freeway is straight and spiritless and wearisome as everything in modern America seems to be, so it is easy to take my eyes from the road and watch the couple through the rearview mirror. She rests the gray straw of her hair on his shoulders. Age has been kinder to Al; his salty beard and bifocals are professorial. Her pouched, pasty face has weathered the years like a forgotten home—strong, rustically beautiful, yet cracked and worn. Their eyes reveal they've been on the road for months. Looking into them is like peering inside the smashed glass panes of an abandoned house—through the windows of their eyes can be seen the faded wallpaper and scuffed floors of their souls.

They both begin talking.

They owned a hotel for seven years, they say, in Wichita, Kansas. It wasn't much of a hotel. You could call it a fleabag. They bought it on a Small Business Administration loan. Most of their long-term tenants worked for three aircraft firms located there. Cigarette smoke fills the back half of the car as Al puffs. When big layoffs came to the aircraft plants, their business fell way off, he says. They lost the hotel.

Eventually, they started traveling, looking for what turns out to be as elusive as the Holy Grail: work.

"I sez, let's go to Albuquerque," says Al, who lights yet another Camel we've offered him. "We had bucks when we left. Our bucks kept dwindling. We had a car, then lost it. We gave away most of our belongings then. That's when we started hitchhiking. That was one year ago. If you would have told me we'd be doing this, I'd never have believed you. Now, we wind up sleeping under bridges or in the open. We take turns staying awake, so no one can sneak up on us. When we started out, I wouldn't let her hitchhike. We'd get up the bus fare. She'd ride and I'd hitch."

Betty adds, "When we see it's not going to work in a town, we go somewhere else."

In the past year, they've run the gauntlet. Dallas. Las Vegas. In Amarillo, Texas, they tell of walking to twenty-seven motels and filling out applications at each one. In Oklahoma City, Al says he did get a temporary job as a construction laborer, but it didn't last long. They say they just spent six unsuccessful job-hunting months in Tulsa, living at a mission run by the Catholic church.

"We wallpapered that town," Al shouts over the grind of a passing semi. "We left the day before yesterday. I wants to work, dammit! That's the Gospel. We've never been on welfare. We've never gotten food stamps. Nothing is beneath us. We'll wash floors. We'll clean shit bowls. We never made a lot. Maybe $15,000 a year, at the most. We don't need much. Just a place to stay.

"The final straw happened the other day. I applied for a job. In the interview, the lady sez I had plenty of experience. The next day on the phone, she sez 'I'll tell you the real reason you didn't get the job.' She sez, 'Look, I'll say I never told you this, but you're over the hill. You're too old. You should try for something else.' "

Anger from an experience like this comes out in many ways. Betty blames minorities.

"The boat people should be shipped back where they came from," says Betty. "In Las Vegas, we saw they had jobs in the hotels. We couldn't get hired. Do you see them out here on the streets? No. They take the jobs."

Betty isn't alone in her anger. In Detroit, an Asian-American mistaken for a Japanese national was bludgeoned to death in a bar by two unemployed autoworkers. "Because of you, motherfucker, we're out of work!" one of the men was reported to have screamed before savaging him with a baseball bat.

Al doesn't offer an opinion on any of this. He just shrugs his shoulders and says they've survived by working at what he calls the "slave markets," day-labor pools; by selling blood plasma; living in missions.

"I hate those missions," says Betty. "They put you down all the time. After a while, you start to wonder if it's true. They want to have power over you."

They're placing all hope on finding work this summer.

"The winters are tough. I don't wants Mouse to spend another winter out here. Maybe I'll send her to one of the kids. We'll play it by ear."

The children and grandchildren. A forbidden subject. A bedrock of silence ensues when we inquire about them. They'll not elaborate. Either they are too proud to ask them for help, or there's a deep family rift. The mere mention of their kids brings pain to their eyes.

They seem happy, though. In the front seat, our tempers flare at each other after several months of road fatigue. Al and Betty try to calm us. They say they've learned to not waste precious energy arguing over problems born of their own tiredness or frustration. It saps them for the real fight, they say, and that is to get out of this fix. In the days we knew them, they never had a harsh exchange.

We continually pass lone hitchhikers marching down the shoulder, many dozens of miles from anything that could be called civilization. Many men in the missions tell of walking as much as a hundred miles at a crack because no one will pick them up. That's why so many wind up on the freights.

We pass an especially pitiful man dragging an army duffle bag, hobbling west down the shoulder like a wounded turtle, twenty miles from the last town. The image of his face, a skull covered with skin, knives our guts. In all the months we've been doing this, we have not gotten used to seeing men like him. We cannot fit him in, and blow past. Al winces. "I feel sorry for every one for them," he says, looking back over his shoulder.

Sagebrush and desolate mountains of New Mexico roll past. The sun sets. Darkness comes, and we are in Arizona.

Freeways are too perfect. Interstates, designed to get you places with unholy speed, are fine if you have a destination. If you are jobless, they just quicken the journey from nowhere to nowhere.

It's too late to pull into Tucson at the hour we near it,

because it would be difficult to find a safe place to sleep—one of the hardest tasks facing those on the road. An error in judgment can cost dearly, especially in evil sections of town. So we decide on the desert. After an hour of hunting near Saguaro National Monument, we find a rutted old jeep trail leading off to a black vacuum.

The doors slam. We're surrounded by the night world. All around, lofty saguaro cactus rise out of the dimness, standing over us like a group of big wizards who have important things to say. We listen, hear, and seem close to seeing the ruby. In the valley below, miles distant, the lights of Tucson sparkle.

Betty wanders off, while we urinate in the middle of the road. The dust swallows the liquid. Over the hill, a pack of coyotes howl at the rising moon.

"Every time the chips are down, something good happens. And I'm not a praying man," says Al, looking off into the heavens laced with clouds of stars. "We've met some good people. We're trying to maintain ourselves. We're not thieves. We've never stolen. Sure, I had renters and did some things. I would take what the traffic would bear. A guy comes in with a tie . . . I'd hit him for twelve bucks a night. But that's all. Nothing worse. Maybe by keeping a few good virtues, good luck has come our way. As long as I have Mouse, I'll be okay."

Betty returns. "We don't know where we are going and when this will end. Times will get better. I believe that." They slump in the back seat, falling asleep in each other's arms.

Come morning, they're embraced in the same position. In Tucson, we drive them around and they apply for jobs at every motel that will let them.

Halfway through the day, a man who owns a small 1940s-vintage motel on the Tucson–Benson Highway tells them to return if they have no luck by evening. He'll let them

Al and Betty wake up in the desert outside of Tucson.

have a room in exchange for painting and yard work around the place, apparently a barely profitable operation with its scant twenty or so rooms in two squat buildings.

Al comes back smiling.

"This is entirely different than Tulsa!" he pronounces. "People are being nicer!"

After unsuccessfully applying at more motels through the afternoon, we return the couple to the Tucson–Benson Highway. They're ecstatic. This is the best luck they've had in months. Betty talks about how she can get a hot plate and cook. Al says he can use the room as a home base to do some serious job hunting.

The cheerful motel owner tells Al and Betty to wait a minute, so he can check with his wife to see which room to give them.

Minutes later, the man returns. He no longer smiles.

"Sorry, I can't help you," he says. "My wife says we can't support everybody who comes through looking for help. She's says we've been doing too much of that. The answer is no."

Al and Betty retreat into the car. Betty bites her lip.

"We never get our hopes up," says Betty. "This kind of thing has happened before."

Al tries one last motel before calling it quits for the day.

"Wait here, Mouse. I'll be back quick. It's going to be another no." Al returns in less than thirty seconds.

"I'll hit the slave market tomorrow," he says sharply. The couple goes off to spend the night at the Salvation Army. This Sally has a three-day limit, so if they don't find work in a few days, they'll hit another town.

Maybe Phoenix. Maybe somewhere in California. They don't know.

People too proud to sleep inside a mission will pull up to the curb in front of the Tucson Sally and spend the night in their cars. They park here because it's safe, and a neutral ground where the police will not hassle you. The mission helped almost twenty-nine thousand people in 1982, says its director.

This evening, there are cars from Pennsylvania, several Midwestern states, and Texas. Al and Betty go inside. We bed down in the car, but sleep eludes us.

It's midnight, and hot. A woman taps on the window and informs us she is hearing voices from outer space coming from her teeth. She sits on the lawn and chants. An old Chevy pulls up and joins us in line. A bent woman, at least sixty, closes the door and walks up. She is lonely. Also quite drunk.

She lost her Texas home, she tells us, so she went to Modesto, California, to live with her daughter. That didn't work out, so now she just drives aimlessly around the country.

"You gotta be out here to know how tough it is," she says, slurring. "All I need is a house. That's all. I don't want any he'p. I can work."

She walks back to the Chevy and passes out in the back seat.

We drive north to Phoenix, the town in the sun that hates the poor. To get rid of the homeless, the city declared garbage city property to prevent scavenging; it rezoned neighborhoods to evict virtually every mission and soup kitchen; and made it against the law to lie down or sleep on public property.

For us, at least, it's another Houston. A cop is waiting at the road leading into town. He stops us, ostensibly because of a loose rear license plate. He is not as mean as the Houston cop, though.

In town, men with packs are everywhere. We follow the direction they walk. We end up at the St. Vincent de Paul

Society, a warehouse full of dozens of beds opened by the charity in response to the city's crackdown on the poor.

The evening lineup is going strong when we arrive. Several hundred stand outside the warehouse, waiting to get a bed for the night.

A couple approaches. They fit in with much of the crowd about as well as born-again Christians at a Reno brothel. He's at least five decades old; she is about the same age, and her striped dress is sharp and pretty as she is.

"We had it good. Suddenly, the roof fell in." These are the first words out of Walt's mouth as he gets behind us in line. He is so new at this he is still telling everyone he meets about their problems.

He worked seventeen years as a trucker for a firm in Colorado Springs, Colorado. Pat, his second wife, tells us she worked for the government as a secretary in a social services agency. He raised three children, who now have their own children.

Then, the trucking firm went bankrupt. Pat lost her federally funded job when social program budgets were cut. For two years, they say, they were told no when applying for jobs. Meanwhile, the Denver area was crushed with a multitude of unemployed Easterners, people much younger, which made job hunting harder. About ten days ago, they lost their rented trailer.

Frantic, they left.

Now, they're on the run from poverty. The couple is too embarrassed to tell their children they're living on the streets.

On the way here, their 1974 station wagon broke down in Flagstaff. They called the police, who took them to a mission. The mission gave them an alternator, worth $30. For payment, Walt painted the inside of the shelter for three days. Still, that wasn't enough, he feels. "When I get some money, I'm going to pay them back," he says.

"We got here with ninety-eight cents in our pocket," says Pat. "We sold blood right away to get a quarter tank of gas. We haven't gotten food stamps, though. We won't do that unless we really have to. I guess sometimes you have to swallow your pride and accept help."

"I'm not bragging. We're good workers," says Walt. He thumbs his belt buckle shaped like a tractor trailer. "We just got to get lucky. Right now, the minimum wage sounds good. Three years ago, I wouldn't have said that. When we get a job, it'll be okay. We'll hang on to it real tight. We're going to try our best here in Phoenix. I don't know where we'll go if we don't find it here."

Says Pat, "The only time we got down was when we were sleeping in the car. It's hard to wash. How do you look for a job when you're dirty and stink? That's the hardest thing—keeping clean."

"Finding a safe place to sleep is tough, too," says Walt. "When we got here five days ago, we slept in a twenty-four-hour restaurant parking lot. We figured that would be safe. But the police kicked us out."

"I feel like a runaway senior citizen," says Pat. "We have to start all over."

The line begins moving.

"I'm at an age," says Walt, "when I'm supposed to be getting ready for retirement. Look at me."

Before they are swallowed inside the big building, we holler wishes of good fortune. We drive off, wondering what fate awaits two people who so well match the stereotype of a kindly aunt and uncle.

We are running out of road. It leads west, into California.

Warehouse home to the homeless, St. Vincent de Paul Society, Phoenix.

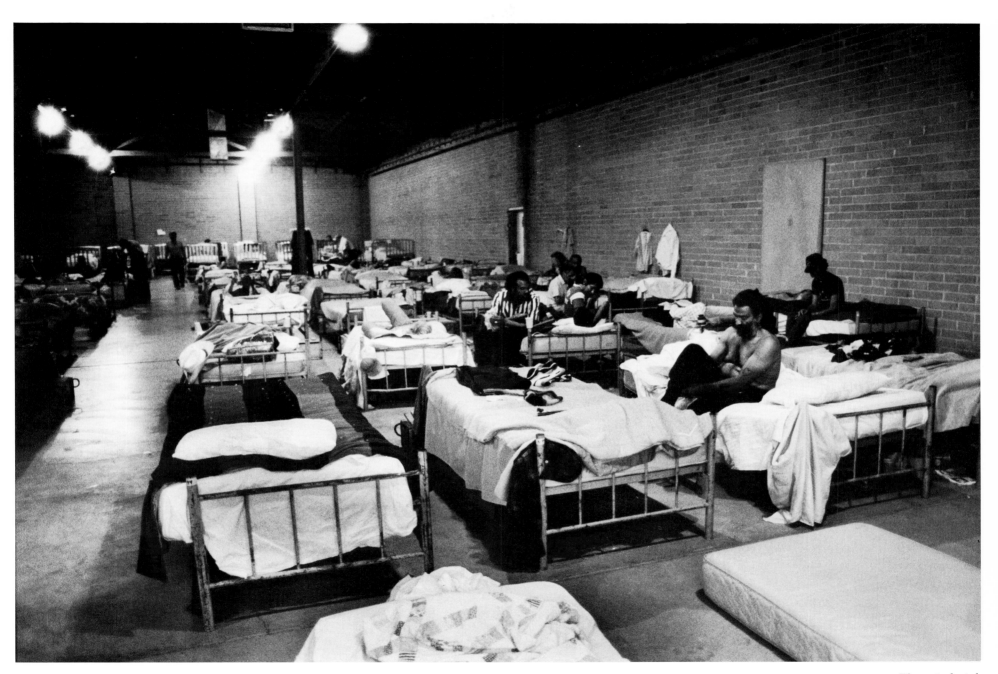

Phoenix hotel.

Jobless couple sleeping in car
camped on banks of Colorado River,
Yuma, Arizona.

This man earns seventy-five cents
a day collecting aluminum cans to sell
at a recycling center.

Camp, Yuma, Arizona.

Chapter 12: **THE ROAD TO PARADISE**

*"Buddy, please, my kids . . . look at them. They're starvin'.
Ain't eat in two days. I've got enough gas money to get me
where I'm goin'. When I get them to my mother-in-law's in
Sacramento, they'll eat. And there's work there. But I can't
buy food now. I won't make it. You gotta help. See these
tools? Cheap. Wanna buy some clothes? Here, look in the
suitcase. Tell you what, I'll sell the suitcase. Anything."*

In the back seat, three small children sob uncontrollably.
That's hungry crying coming from those kids. John, the gas
station attendant, can't take it anymore. The wailing haunts
his soul. He buys the rusting tools. Pays the man more than
they're probably worth. Even gives the family the hamburger
he'd just bought for dinner.

John sees a lot at his place, just off Interstate 40, on
the outskirts of Needles—the first service station you come
to when you cross the Colorado River from Arizona into
California. Needles, a dusty rail stop of tacky storefronts,
was the first California city most Dust Bowl refugees saw
when they came over Route 66 in the 1930s.

"We see a lot from Pennsylvania, New York, and West
Virginia . . . coal miners, mostly, from there," says John.

"They go into Barstow. From there, into the Central Valley,
or Los Angeles. Most come out here hoping to stay for a time
with a relative before making do on their own.

"People will pull in here from the East and Texas . . . at
the same time, people leaving California will pull in. They
get talking to each other. The ones heading west say there's
a lot of work in California. The ones going east say there's
a lot of work in Texas. They're all chasing dreams, rumors."

John kicks back his chair, throws his feet on his desk,
looking out the window at the gas pumps shimmering in
the Mojave Desert heat, and to the road beyond. He points
to an Ohio car toting a moving trailer just pulling off the
interstate. Moments later, two open-bed trucks motor past,
piled eight feet deep in bicycles, trunks, tools, and furniture.

"All day long you see them go by. After a while, you
harden yourself to it. You say no when they want to sell
stuff. There were a lot of people on the road in the late
sixties. Everyone was brothers then. Now, people are scared
to death. It's not the same anymore. These people are
desperate."

John helps a customer.

Down the road, the two open-bed trucks come to a stop

in the shade of a live oak in the center of Needles. The engines inside the dented hoods crackle and snap as they cool.

A shy woman drives the rear truck. A sleeping blond girl, maybe nine years old, naps in a fetal position on the front seat next to the woman. A boy of twelve rides in the front truck, with Dad. Dad, a bearded, stocky man, clad in grease-stained jeans, carefully feels the rear axle of his wife's truck.

"Isn't hot, so it must be holding," he mutters to no one in particular. Bearing gave out a hundred miles back, and he had to replace it on the spot, he explains. He introduces himself as Ron Wright. Came from Dallas. Worked for a company there for a year, until it went broke. Went from living in a house to sleeping in a trailer. When their money started drying up, they loaded the trucks and looked for work in Georgia. Then the money ran out. Ron decided to go work for his father, in Paradise, California, a small town in the northern Central Valley.

"Goin' slow, but we're gettin' there. Everything is here— my work, my home," he says, patting the load lashed together tighter than a hay bale. "I'm a mechanic. My dad always wanted me to work for him, but he felt I could make more money other places. Didn't know what to do. I give up on everybody else. So I'll work for him.

"Gotta go," he says. "Hell, we're in California. Gotta get to Barstow, quick, where some money's being wired to us. Gotta get to Paradise."

Ron turns his engine over. Marilyn follows. The clatter of the V-8s is drowned out by the guttural jabbering of six nearby Santa Fe units at the head of a westbound train in the railyard. The trucks wheel down the highway, toward the setting sun. The train follows.

West.

Evening . . . a special hour in the desert. The world cools. Darkness advances. Horizons become limitless. The sun dips behind the Dead Range overshadowed by wisps of purple cirrus clouds . . . but continues to send rays streaming around the peaks. Westbound travelers are showered with a golden light. It's the magic hour, alive with hope and promise, when anything is possible. The gilded light reaches out like the gentle touch of a lover's hands, caressing travelers' souls, calling them on. At such a moment, as anyone who's driven in the desert knows, you are blinded to everything but the shadows of the mountains and the dim outline of the road.

The trucks and train vanish from sight.

The world is good. Welcome to California.

A rubber tramp's camp, the Central Valley.

Hoeing sugar beets, Firebaugh, California. The Central Valley.

Chapter 13: **THE BIG VALLEY**

The Santa Fe freight with its yellow units plunges like a steel centipede over the edge of the Tehachapi Mountains, the wheels ringing on curves. Roger Williams, riding on the back of the bucking train, gazes far below at a golden plain stretching off to a shadowy horizon. This is the rich land he has heard so much about, a place of palm trees and fruit orchards, the great Central Valley of California.

The geometrically perfect outline of Bakersfield shimmers at the base of the mountain. It's a sweltering place, a transplanted version of a lethargic Texas town, the southernmost major population center in a string of valley cities. Many of its residents are migrants or their descendants, who fled the Dust Bowl seeking a better life. When the train clears the mountains and stops here, Williams jumps off, hurrying to the catch-out place in the yard near the mission. He waits for a northbound that will take him up the valley through Fresno, Modesto, Stockton, Sacramento, and beyond to Marysville, He squints from the glare of the setting sun, adding wrinkles to those already around his eyes, gripping his suitcase as if waiting for a bus. He keeps a nervous eye on dozens of others who've recently jumped off freights coming in from the south.

This is a rough yard, so the word goes. Under a bridge, the sight of a dozen hairy, growling characters with big knives strapped on their sides is enough to convince Williams that danger exists. For safety, the former welder, who is white, has teamed with an unemployed black man. The black man fears groups of white hoboes. Williams fears groups of black hoboes. "Funny what you'll do to survive," says the black man.

"I went through Texas and New Mexico looking for work, and there was nothing," Williams mutters. "Same way everywhere you go. Real bad." He looks at his traveling companion. "We don't have a dime between us."

Williams sits on an inverted can to keep his slacks and checkered shirt clean. He rolls his last cigarette from a pouch of Bugler tobacco. When he gets to Marysville, he hopes to pick peaches in farm-labor camps. He's heard they might rip him off, but it doesn't matter.

"I'm going to work them, anyway," he shouts over the thunder of passing southbound units. "Our only hope is to get to Marysville. If we make five dollars a day, I'll be happy."

Farming rules the Central Valley.

When the harvest is on, a night and day procession of trucks burdened with overflowing produce barrel down the valley to the canneries and processing houses.

A smart man down on his luck will watch the side of

the road for places where bumps cause vegetables to fall off the rigs. During the onion harvest, you can eat a lot of free onion soup. If a man is hungry enough, of course, he can raid the fields at night. When the crops are in, starvation is impossible in the valley.

It's hard to imagine how much food is grown in this basin 350 miles long and 50 miles wide. As flat as Kansas, it's nestled between the snowcapped Sierra on the east and the drier Coast Range on the west. The Central Valley helps California earn its position as the state with the largest agricultural industry in the nation, worth over $13 billion a year in the early 1980s.

Cotton, sugar beets, peaches, pears, tomatoes, almonds, walnuts—just some of the crops grown here. Farm laborers were a vital part of Central Valley farming half a century ago. Now, machines harvest many crops, such as cotton and tomatoes.

But machines cannot do all chores. They cannot properly hoe sugar beets or cotton, pick peaches. Backs are still needed. Such jobs are traditionally shunned by the middle class. The work appeals to desperate men, eager to make a few bucks. In the Great Depression, they were "Okies." In the boom years of the fifties and sixties, they were Mexican nationals. Today, they are still mainly illegal immigrants, but they are being joined by the new poor.

Some farmers hire their own workers; others contract with labor camps. The camps hire the men, then sell them like slaves. Some camps are fair, but others are bitter hellholes. The worst seem to be run by owners who take buses into Fresno, Bakersfield, or Los Angeles to pick up men on skid row. These camps don't want rubbertramps, because they can leave at will. Farmers pay camp owners a fee over and above the federal minimum of $3.35 an hour for each man. Some camps in turn pay the men the minimum, but deduct expenses, such as room and board, which was as high as $20 a day in one camp.

For this fee, men have the privilege of sleeping in a barn, eating gruel that doesn't cost more than a buck to make. Want a cup and blanket? That's $15 extra. Want a Coke with lunch? That costs a buck, deducted from your pay. Don't like the prices? Walk eight miles to town.

In one camp, a man who detests smoking was charged for eight packs of cigarettes. On payday, the camp owner doled out checks with a .38 Ruger perched on his desk. With that kind of persuasion, says the man, you don't argue.

Yet, they come.

Word of farm work travels far. From Mexico, they come. From Middle America, men who made as much as $20,000 a year at one time come too, by car, by freight, by thumb.

Butch gazes out the window with slowly understanding eyes. He winces and coughs from lung-searing fumes seeping through the rickety floor of the 1950s-vintage school bus built for humans the size of fourth-graders. It churns and bucks, slamming his head against the low ceiling, jarring him into a state of semiwakefulness.

The steady bongo beat of an unraveling retreaded tire drumming inside the left wheel well is added fuel for his headache. Butch desperately wants to puke, but refrains. He clutches the window ledge, eyes fixed on the night.

Central Valley towns, still asleep at this inhospitable hour, pass in the darkness—places like Crow's Landing, Gustine, Los Banos.

Between these islands of humanity is nothing, or at least it appears so in the darkness. These blank places are fields full of cotton, fruit orchards, tomatoes. Corporate farms. Mega-acres that produce megabucks, at least in his eyes. The land is rich; indeed, as wealthy as he is poor.

After three hours of lurching, color comes to the predawn horizon. With it, the endless sugar beet fields outside Firebaugh come into view. We are nearly there.

Butch's head once again rattles against the roof with a

loud *clang*, his plump butt squishing down on the seat. He snarls bitterly. The muttering matures into full-fledged, fist-waving screaming, a torrent of vicious obscenities directed at the sugar beets.

Mexican nationals still trying to sleep at the front of the bus shout in Spanish and shake their fists in return, telling him to shut up.

Butch ignores the complaints, continuing his tirade. He tells the captive audience his utter contempt for those beets and everything else that's happened to him.

Butch is disgusted with having cultivated them all week long; he's sick of being wakened at 2:30 A.M., three hours after his body collapses on a rusty cot in a blistering hot barn that sleeps one hundred others; he's sick of having diarrhea and the farts, a condition he attributes to greasy camp food.

God, he doesn't want to be here, he whines.

His companions try to calm their red-faced friend as the bus jerks to a halt next to a sugar beet field.

His two buddies aren't any happier with being here, either. But they're desperate for cash. If they don't raise $300 within one week, they'll lose their rented home in a tidy Modesto neighborhood. After endless weeks of unsuccessful job hunting, the men had no choice. They had to come work for this farm labor contractor. Black Bill was once an $18-an-hour construction foreman before the firm for which he worked thirteen years went out of business. Butch was a cook. Short Bill was laid off from his federally funded county parks job.

Still moaning, Butch is hurried off the bus by the field boss who wears a Panama hat like a crown. The trio jumps onto the soft, damp earth, facing the field stretching to the eastern horizon where the sun rises out of the haze. The Coast mountains command the western sky. Dampness strikes the skin like frost. Butch and the others promise we will beg for the chill of morning before long.

"You just wait and see," Butch tells us new-timers. "Pick them weeds for one hour. You'll wish you never came here."

Like rifles being thrown into recruits' arms, hoes are thrust at us. We shuffle between neat rows of dew-soaked beets that glisten like reflectors down the center strip of a nighttime highway.

The field boss commands that work begin.

Hoes attack the earth, rising and falling in rhythmic, mechanical succession like pump arms on oil wells. Weeds as big as saplings that refuse to yield to the hoe or are next to beets must be yanked with both hands. We labor hard, but fall behind. The Mexican nationals outhoe our group of eight Americans. The Mexicans are perhaps the hardest workers I have ever seen.

They are good, and we are bad at this. The field boss demands perfection, ordering us to run back scores of yards to get finger-tall weeds missed by accident. The pace is furious. You must hoe while almost running at a trot. Factory work pales in comparison.

The sun climbs.

Butch vents his anger on the weeds, hacking with a vengeance, his potbelly quivering with each chop. He hopes for lunchtime, which seems near. But it's not even 9 A.M., a man sings out from several rows over. The field boss drives the crew like a team of horses down dreadfully eternal rows.

As promised, the modest chill of morning quickly turns to the boisterous heat of day. Beets wilt. Humidity from the plants billows in our faces. Our minds numb. Time is suspended. Workers on the flanks are distorted by shimmering heat waves and the sting of sweat in our eyes.

Feeling leaves our arms. Black Bill appears ready to collapse. His hoe is all that holds him up between listless scrapings. Short Bill eases his misery by fantasizing about pork chops and women. Thinking aloud, he makes love; then he cooks the chops, savoring each bite.

"We'll get a six-pack of cold beer when we get home," he

Short Bill, Butch, and black Bill. Dinnertime at the farm labor camp, inside the sweltering barn.

announces. "I'll put some pepper on them poke chops and we'll have a real good dinner."

Butch is troubled by such dreams. "Bill," he sighs in a plaintive voice. "You know we can't afford beer. We've got to get enough rent money together or we'll be thrown out."

The ensuing silence is broken when the field boss orders a lunch break. "Lunch-ee! Lunch-ee! We got Gomez sand-weech!" he shouts sarcastically. "Cheese san-weech! Bologna san-weech! Gomez special!"

"Yeah . . . Gomez special," grouses a sour-faced construction worker from Alabama. "That means it's three days old."

The bologna is brown and green. The cheese sandwich is wadded like a doughball used for carp bait. Sandwiches fly in the ditch, but Butch is hungry and gulps his. The only decent food is a golf-ball-sized apple.

Lunch ends all too soon. Hoes resume scratching the cement of sun-baked earth. The nightmare ends when the field boss's watch creeps to quitting time.

Each man has hoed at least four miles of beets and pulled at least ten thousand weeds today. We shamble into the bus for a three-hour ride back to camp.

Once there, the three men drag their floppy bodies from the bus. They climb the creaking stairs of the weathered two-story barn they've called home all week. As they near the door, a hot blast of air assaults their noses—smelling of vomit, urine, and dirt.

"We swept it, but couldn't get the dust up," Black Bill apologizes. "We gave up trying to clean it."

Butch, sunburned and puffed in the face, figures he's had about fifteen hours' sleep in the past five days. Because the barn is so hot, it's impossible to doze off before midnight.

They sit in the shade behind the camp, next to an irrigation ditch flanking a tomato field. Crows chortle and cavort in a distant clump of trees. Butch swishes at flies, and explains how much they're in debt.

"After we pay the $300 rent, another $180 is going to be due, and then we still have a $71 utility bill. We're thinking about selling the furniture."

After a week of hoeing, the men want their pay so they can return to civilization, give their landlord some money, and look for better work.

The three walk to the office to ask for the checks. An argument ensues. The camp owner swears, and does not want to pay them until they work one more day. After a fiery debate, he begrudgingly writes the checks.

They emerge from the office, standing in brilliant sunlight, next to the row of crippled buses, and look at their pay. Their jaws unhinge. Gasps fill the air.

At $3.35 an hour, each grossed $134 for sixty hours. After deductions, Butch cleared $56.52; Black Bill, $53.97; Short Bill, $49.54. Their net is between 82 and 94 cents an hour.

Black Bill holds out his blistered palms and stares in disbelief at the hands that once built $180,000 condominiums.

"Damn!" shouts Butch.

He slaps his baseball cap against his knee. A cloud of dust rises from his pants and is carried away by the wind. We leave them and move on to another camp.

It doesn't look like much, this village of a dozen graying shanties strutting up on the treeless plain, isolated and exposed like ships on the open sea—but the sea here is boundless cotton fields.

We walk up to the camp, west of Pixley, seeking work. While we wait for the owner under the shade of the only tree in sight for miles, big-band music from a Tulare oldies station filters out of one of the shacks. The air is abuzz with squadrons of flies. Wind chants softly through the fluffy cotton field across a rushing irrigation ditch.

So you want work, says the shrewd-looking owner as he approaches. We lie and say we are down on our luck, and need any work, please. Our unshaven looks, tattered clothes tell him we are poor. But he peers in our eyes, and it seems they make him suspicious. We fear our eyes say we have been eating well and make good money and are not desperate enough to be here. "Pay is the minimum, board $12, and we charge 80 cents for a roll of toilet paper," he tells us, anyway. Take it or leave it.

He escorts us to one of the shanties, assigned to be our home. He says in his thirty years as a contractor, he's never seen so many new-timers from the East. It's a buyer's market, and he likes that.

"They're coming in on the freights out of the South looking for work. These guys want to earn a buck to earn a buck, not to buy booze."

We're ordered to clean the premises. The hovel's crooked door slams behind us.

Human turds, deposited by the previous occupant and fossilized by heat, litter the floor. The mattress is stained yellow. The interior of the dented wood-burning stove has been colonized by a half-dozen graceless black widow spiders.

The owner returns, ignoring complaints of low wages and uncivilized accommodations.

"It all depends how hungry you are," he says.

Move on up the valley. Hitchhiking produces no rides. Burn shoe leather. Pick 'em up and put 'em down, down a desolate Merced County road, under that god-awful hot sun. The heat bakes your mind as crisp as deep-fried pork fat. Night comes, and with it, a cool Pacific breeze escapes over the Coast Range and slinks to the valley floor, massaging your face with its cool palms. The air is flavored with the smell of the sea, dust of the land, and tingles the lungs with each breath.

Hungry? Satisfy the pit in your stomach by running into a field and snatching up a handful of tomatoes. Roadside ditches harbor hordes of humming crickets and katydids. Occasionally, a car speeds past, the roar of the engine echoing across cotton fields. The embers of the taillights burn dimly, framed by the wispy outlines of ever present distant mountains.

Come morning, we find Bob Hamilton, his thin frame bopping up and down, walking into a camp near Newman. He just trod fifteen miles from the camp where Butch and his two friends work. As if to prove his trek, he lifts his foot, poking his index finger through the sole.

"Now, my shoes are falling apart," he says gravely, squatting on the ground. "I had my own business . . . now I'm getting the business." He owned a remodeling firm in Kansas City, but lost it when orders fell off. "I looked for work, and wound up hitting the rails and coming out here."

Still, he is determined. He looks up at us with eager eyes. "I'm going to save enough money to start another business again someday," he announces.

We leave him leaning against the shady side of a building, contemplating this prospect.

Across a tomato field spattered with the glowing red jewels of ripe fruit is a compound of cinder-block buildings surrounded by a twelve-foot chain-link fence topped with barbed wire. An armed guard patrols the perimeter. A row of men sit in faded automobile seats lined against one of the block huts. Their heads are bowed.

Dust clouds erupt from our drowsy feet as we near the office of this camp near Mendota. The boss barks he's not hiring.

Back outside, we sit in one of the car seats, trying to strike up a conversation. Silence greets us. The men's eyes remain bolted to the ground in a druglike stupor. We walk into the shower house to wash the dirt from our faces. Next to the toilets, three men roll dice, throwing dollar bills back

Bob Hamilton.

Mike Sienienkiewiczi
and James Brown.

and forth. One man tries to speak, but only grunts emerge from his throat.

Through the back door, a fourth man runs in, howling wildly. The dice rollers ignore the howler as he prances over the game and vanishes through the front entrance.

A strange place, indeed. We hurriedly leave and head for a Los Banos camp, where we find two guys who look like they've just walked off a tennis court. James Brown and Mike Sienienkiewiczi introduce themselves, the latter tripping out his roller-coaster name in a heavy Jersey accent.

It turns out they also just came from the Mendota camp, which Brown describes with a shudder as "Auschwitz."

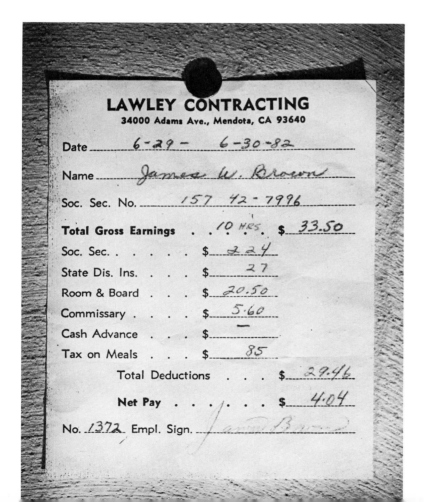

LAWLEY CONTRACTING
34000 Adams Ave., Mendota, CA 93640

Date __6-29- 6-30-82__

Name __James W. Brown__

Soc. Sec. No. __157 42 - 7996__

Total Gross Earnings . . __10 HRS__. $ __33.50__

Soc. Sec. . . . . . $ __2.24__

State Dis. Ins. . . . $ __27__

Room & Board . . . $ __20.50__

Commissary . . . . $ __5.60__

Cash Advance . . . $ __—__

Tax on Meals . . . $ __85__

   Total Deductions . . . $ __29.46__

   Net Pay . . . . . . $ __4.04__

No. __1372__ Empl. Sign. __James Brown__

They spent all their money job hunting in Los Angeles, where they'd flown to from their native New Jersey. They were sitting in a coffee shop talking about their financial problems. A man who overheard them told of a way to make money. Just go to a particular street corner, he said, and wait. A labor contractor's bus came and brought them to the Mendota camp.

Once at the camp, they found it difficult to leave (they and sixty other men were charged $3 each for an eight-mile bus ride into town for one hour each week). Brown produces a receipt that shows he netted $4.04 for ten hours hoeing cotton. He gnaws on a peach he'd pocketed from the day's picking as he sits with his buddy in the shade of a tree.

"We also picked garlic. They pay you a dollar fifty a bucket," says Brown. "You can only do about five buckets a day. It just about pays your board. The only cotton I ever saw before this was Fruit of the Loom. I'm a city boy. After I get out of this, my farm days are through."

"They got you all figured out," adds Sienienkiewiczi, a trucker by trade. "They know we need the money. The only reason we're here is that it's better than the missions."

Says Brown: "I miss my job back in New York. I want it back. I like nine dollars an hour."

The San Joaquin River is the mother of the lower half of the valley, flowing rich and deep through the delta farmland before it spills into Suisun Bay, an arm of San Francisco Bay. The air is weighted with the sound of swamp fauna in a state-run camp on the banks on the river. Unlike Houston, there are plenty of inexpensive or even free places to camp in the Central Valley.

"We're seeing more itinerants," ranger Tom Palmquist tells us. "We're a little bit more like the thirties with the Okies. There are more people scratching right now."

James Brown's receipt for ten hours of hoeing cotton.

Shoes that have seen many days in the fields.

The shower at a Mendota camp described by Brown as "Auschwitz."

As we near another camp to the north, we pass a broken-down Chevy slumped at the side of the road. The legs of a man protrude from beneath the frame. A woman sits on a suitcase, holding a grease-covered, crying baby. Two other children chase a dog into a vineyard purple with ripe grapes.

We stop to help. Charley Roberts rolls from underneath, coming up with a burned-out starter motor in one blackened hand, rubbing his goatee with the other.

Roberts tells us he wound up here after he heard a radio report about the need for strawberry pickers in Monterey. He never did that before, he says, but figured he could learn. So he loaded the 1966 Chevy, packed in the family, and hit the road.

When he got to Monterey, the boss man told him they already had plenty of pickers and didn't need any more. He drove the Chevy to this park and made camp. He found several days of construction work—his old trade—in Stockton. It was his first work in one year. Now, he wants to get back to Marysville to work the peach harvest.

He dives back under the car, groaning and struggling with the starter that simply will not work. He had the car towed from the park while he fixed it so he wouldn't have to pay camping fees.

The children watch from a quiet distance while Dad talks to us. Mom smiles and doesn't say much. We offer to take Charley into town for a new starter. We throttle off, leaving his family behind.

Last winter, Roberts says, they survived by eating out of dumpsters. He'd make dumpster runs for vegetables and dented cans behind Marysville supermarkets. Toward the end of winter, Roberts says, six-year-old Ned got terribly ill. "I thought he was going to die, and I was responsible for it," he says.

Roberts once made $20,000 a year, at a job he held since he came home from Vietnam in 1972. "Now, my unemployment is gone. I don't know what I'm going to do," he says.

At the auto parts store, the counterman shakes his head when he looks at the starter. "You're gonna need a solenoid, too, buddy."

Charley's eyes widen, and he peers in his wallet like a wino looking down an empty bottle, wishing there was more.

The counterman, wearing a blue service station shirt and with a pencil behind his ear, looks up the prices. "Let's see, the starter'll be $26.49, and the solenoid . . . uh, that comes with it."

I'm standing nearest the counterman and can see across at the parts book. The solenoid was extra.

Back in our car, Charley tells us that leaves him $4 to get to Marysville. We offer a loan, but he staunchly refuses. Earlier, he told us he has not yet asked for welfare. "I don't want to go there and hassle with them unless I have too," he says.

Eighteen-month-old Christina is still crying when we return. She wipes her nose with a hand dirtied by the car. Jack, seven, hugs the dog, Brandy.

We bend under the car with Charley and watch. He quietly confesses he cannot read. The only thing he knows is manual labor. "I learned concrete. I'll learn something else, if somebody will give me a chance."

He tightens down the last bolt with a force that shakes the whole car. He's anxious to get to Marysville and pick peaches.

Polly, thirty-two, smiles apprehensively when her husband of thirteen years tells her to turn the key in the ignition.

The car roars to life. The children jump and clap. Brandy wags his tail.

"If there's a peach-picking job up there, I'll find me one," says Roberts as he gets in the car. "I always thought you go up instead of down, but picking peaches now sounds up for me."

The Roberts family.

The Roberts family just after Charley gets the car working. Charley stares at his greasy hands.

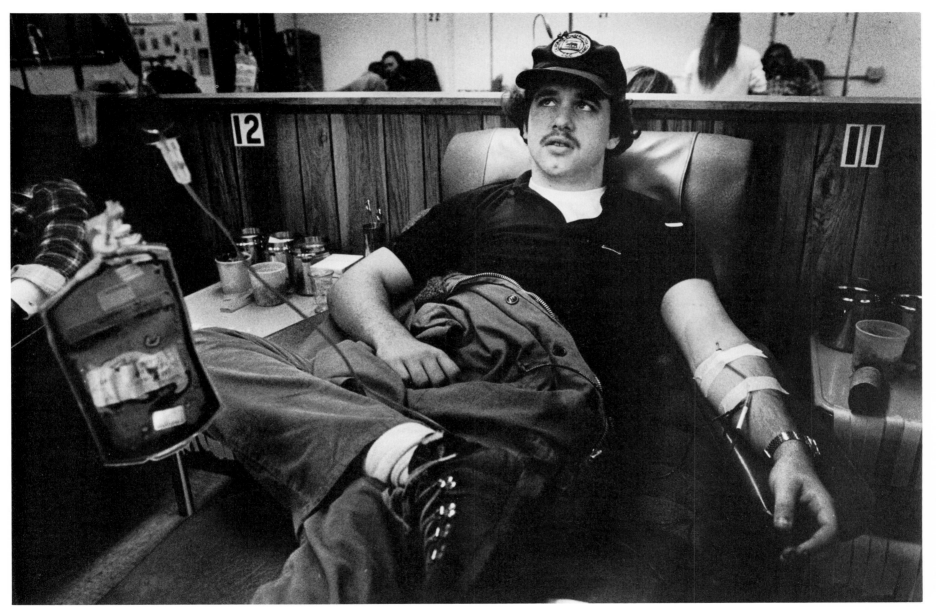

Many of the unemployed sell blood plasma, the clear, beer-colored component of blood. Red and white blood cells are centrifuged out and placed back in the body with a saline solution. The pint of plasma is then sold by the plasma center to a hospital. People can sell plasma twice a week. Prices were as high as $15, but dropped when so many unemployed started selling it, to as low as $7. Here Mike Raynor, twenty-one, gives plasma during the two-hour process. He entered the labor market at a tough time and couldn't find work.

This is how much food they could buy with the $9 Raynor was paid for his plasma. The $1.65 in change will be used for bus fare to look for work.

Raynor and his wife, Wendy, share a tender moment in their cramped apartment in Sacramento.

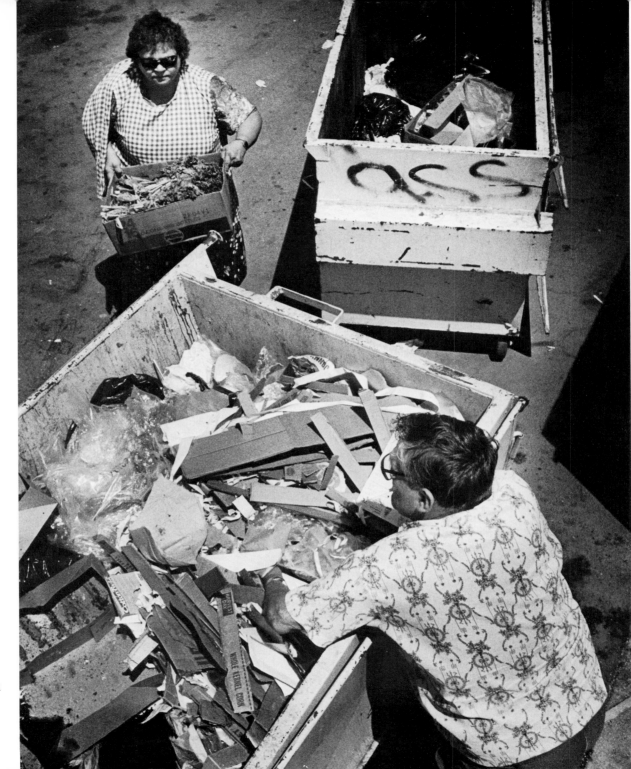

Man collecting food from
a dumpster, Sacramento.

Couple salvages food from
a grocery store dumpster.

Chapter 14: **WINTER**

Clickity clack. Clickity clack.
Lookin' back. Lookin' back.
Where ya' goin'? Where ya' goin'?
Where ya' been? Where ya' been?
Clickity clack. Clickity clack.
Don't come back. Don't come back.

—An old hobo chant

The Southern Pacific's wheels seem to sing this lonely tune, born of steel meshing against steel, exalting the men who made the metal and the men who now ride it. The blurred ground a few feet below, viewed from the rear of our rocking grainer, is hypnotic and seems eternal. In the world of the hobo, this is the way it has always been, and always will be.

In the Stockton yard, hoboes hover over smoking campfires, clustered in groups at the bottom of a treeless gully next to the tracks. Faces blackened with road dirt snap to attention as the train slows to a stop. For some, the long wait for a ride is over, and they run to board. We leap off and enter the jungle.

A boyish youth welcomes us into his camp, offering instant coffee served in soup cans. We demur when we learn it's his last. "So what," he says, emptying the remaining crystals from the jar. "We're all in this together."

We sip the brew and catch the next northbound Western Pacific.

Sunrise in the Oroville rail yard, on the way to Oregon.

The Butte County sheriff's deputy pulls out his nightstick and kicks through the dust and broken glass of the jungle. His face is as hard as the debris beneath his feet. We're ordered to produce identification. He wants to see if we're wanted by the law. Not far from us a man named Tom tries to hop aboard a southbound, which is building air to release its brakes so it can leave. The deputy screams, and herds him together with the two of us and a couple we'd just ridden in with.

Tom, a sheet metal worker unemployed for four months, anxiously eyes the train, whispering his hate for the box-jawed officer and his hate for the system when the deputy saunters off to search for other hoboes. Oregon is a waste of time, he informs us. Just came from there. No work. And where there was work, he was told he was too old at age forty-four. "Being black doesn't help, either," he adds.

"I'm tired of this shit," he says. "You stay nasty and

dirty all the time. And the police are always messing with you."

The officer returns, twirling the nightstick.

"You all listen up now," he says slowly, pausing between each word as if we're too ignorant to understand. "There's too many of you out here. A lot of you congregating like this causes trouble. We want you on a train by sundown. If you are here when I come back, you are all going to jail."

Well before the sundown deadline, big green Burlington Northern units pull into the yard, bound for Klamath Falls, Oregon—"K-Falls" in the jargon of hoboes. The train drops its air, signaling everyone hiding in the weeds. Twenty-five men, a woman, and two dogs materialize from the brush, lugging water jugs and packs, running to catch choice riding places.

It's an icy, tooth-shattering ride as the smoking diesel chariot winds through dozens of tunnels up the Feather River Canyon. After ten eternal hours of highballing, the train pulls in the K-Falls yard at 3 A.M. We're blinded by a spotlight, aimed in our boxcar by a young bull. The shaking bull, hand on his .38, IDs us and tells us if the jail wasn't full, we'd be going there. He promises five days in the slammer if he ever sees us again.

Come daylight, we hike to the Southern Pacific yard, where we find several hoboes scraping spilled rice from beneath grain cars. "Dinner," one blurts out before they run off to cook their find. We sit next to the abandoned icehouse, buffeted by a lunatic wind. Our down coats are about as effective as T-shirts at keeping us warm. Scrawled on the icehouse wall are the words "The coldest winter I ever spent was a summer in K-Falls," written in charcoal by some hobo aping Mark Twain's comment about San Francisco.

Two Mexican nationals dressed for the heat of their native country shiver on the north side of the building, wrapped in thousand-mile blankets. We draw a map of the United States in the sand to show where they are. They whistle in disbelief. We manage to learn they're on their way to pick apples in Washington. We don't need an interpreter to know they're starving. We open tins and give them tuna, which vanishes like a fly down a frog's throat.

Winter rains come to the West Coast, ugly all-day, all-night affairs that pound, pound, pound, relentlessly converting everything to a soaking mess. Winter on much of the West Coast is a damp in-between season of grayness. It's not as mean as its eastern counterpart, with blizzards and such, but is miserable all the same.

The rains savage Portland, Oregon. The new poor with some money hole up in the cheap hotels of the Burnside district: rooms are dank cells with plastic drapes; beds are stained from several decades' accumulation of bodily secretions; old men hack and wheeze; the halls creak with each passing step; downstairs, the owner with a wart on his nose glares, standing beneath the sign that says "No Visitors!"

The penniless who cannot afford the luxury of the Burnside hotels can be found walking through the drizzle, trudging across the Steel Bridge, a railroad crossing spanning the broad Willamette River, returning to their abodes under freeway overpasses on the opposite side.

So, on one side of the river, the "rich" poor live in the soiled hotels, on the other shore, the "poor" poor. It seems the former still have hope; the latter have given up.

A cop we talk to sneers at the homeless living across the river. He's emphatic. "They're bums! They don't wanna work!"

Man on a flatcar, called a "convertible," the Burlington Northern, headed for Klamath Falls, Oregon.

That may be true for some, but not all. The cop, who makes good money, does not seem to want to understand the scale of events that lead to the breakdown of a person. He is making it, they are not, and therefore, he seems to feel, they are lazy and deserve their lifestyle. But what separates us from them?

How many job lines, soup lines, welfare lines do you have to stand in, in a place like Youngstown, before you give up and become like them?

How much humiliation can you take, when it seems the rest of the world is working and you are not?

How many times do you have to be said no to?

How many cold nights do you have to spend like a dog under a bridge?

How many days without food in a quaking boxcar?

How many months of hoping things will get better, until the months turn into a year, and more, until all hope fades?

At some point, these things add up, and the score is ugly. Some people who cannot escape the plunge are consumed, quit fighting. They submit. It seems the only difference between us and the river people is a few dollars in our pockets.

We think of these things as we walk across the Steel Bridge. We come upon Daniel, who looks across the Willamette at the big buildings of downtown from the front "porch" of his shed beneath an Interstate 5 overpass. He walks down to the bank, taking care not to step on the rotting bodies of rats washed ashore, victims of poison in the grain elevator up the river.

He rattles off his story with a boredom that comes from telling it a thousand times before to people who didn't want to hear: A stint with the U.S. Marines. Worked in Alabama, making furniture. Laid off. Went north, to Youngstown, worked loading trucks. Laid off. Hit the road again.

"Everyone said go to Texas. I went to Texas. There ain't nothing there but them labor camps. Came here."

Daniel's traveling days are through. "Fuck it," he says with cutting finality. "Might as well stay put. There's fish in the river. Built the shack with driftwood. All I need is right here. Traveling around don't do no good. Some stopped looking for work, and I can't blame them. It's a job here, a job there, and it don't last. You can't get nowhere. There ain't nothing."

He trudges back to his porch and resumes his watch over the river. It seems he waits for something big to happen.

Our southbound freight hurtles out of Oregon through the night in a hysterical rainstorm; carrying us around the base of snowcapped, 14,000-foot Mount Shasta; back down into the Central Valley, toward Sacramento. The whirring wheels are dimly visible from our wretched perch on the rear of a grainer. The wind spits rain in at us as if we're sitting on the bow of a speedboat racing across a stormy lake. We're soaked to our underwear. Two stocky men and a blond woman on the grainer in front of ours are also having a bad go of it. On the car behind, a man expresses his feelings by howling like a wolf over the clatter.

Like fleas on a dog's backside, the train is alive with hoboes, coming from nowhere, bound for nowhere.

Daniel.

Couple in a boxcar, on a train bound for Oregon.

Southern Pacific yard, Klamath Falls, Oregon.

Couple sleeps next to yard, Klamath Falls, Oregon.

Hoboes on the street, Klamath Falls, Oregon.

Sid, an unemployed lumberman, lives under this bridge in Klamath Falls, Oregon.

Jesus as a hobo. Portland, Oregon,

Hobo jungle under bridge across the Willamette River, Portland, Oregon.

A man's home under a bridge, Portland, Oregon.

A young couple and Marie, in the abandoned power plant.

Torrents of rainwater tumble through gaping holes in the roof of an abandoned power plant. A flashlight exposes rats splashing and swimming in the cellar, visible twelve feet below through manhole-sized cavities chewed in the ancient concrete floor.

Marie, aged beyond her fifty-seven years, wraps herself in a shawl and walks bent, through the darkness, to a fire in the dry corner of the building, careful not to plunge through one of the holes to the rats below. She hugs her husband Teddy, a nervous man who fidgets with the fire when it doesn't need tending. One dozen sleeping bags begin to stir as the others waken. Marie makes toast for some of them.

"Praise the Lord, it's cold!" she hollers, holding her pale hands over the broken shopping cart functioning as a grill.

Marie and Teddy have lived here the longest, coming one month ago when the rains started. The others wandered in over the past few weeks, men like Steve Elias, a laid-off shipbuilder from Seattle, or David Bentley, a twenty-year-old kid from back East who rode a freight here. They formed an informal family, dividing the smelly cavern into bedrooms, sharing cooking, wood-gathering, and fire-tending chores.

The others slowly gather around the blaze. Fourteen saddened mimelike faces shine in the firelight. It is their last morning in this home. When daylight comes to the gray skies of Sacramento, they must leave. The California state police who found them here yesterday ordered them out by sunrise.

"Our living here isn't hurting anybody," Marie says. Her voice is swallowed like a rifle shot by the black walls of the tomb. "Who else wants this building other than the skunks and rats?"

No matter. The law's the law, and you can't camp on state-owned property, the police told her yesterday. "We're not coldhearted," says the boss cop. "We're forced into this position. It's a tough goddang world out there."

Tough, for sure. Teddy and Marie have learned. Their education began one year ago when Teddy was laid off from a sawmill in Colorado. After working at a Montana church, the couple began traveling by bus through the West, shipping boxes of their worldly possessions along with them—pots, pans, books, clothes. A priest in Nevada suggested they come to Sacramento. Here, their money ran out.

"We figured welfare would help us when we got here. Nobody would help us. I paid taxes all the years I worked," says Teddy as he packs their belongings. "They say there's work. *Bullshit!* You can't buy a job! The rich are getting richer; the poor, poorer."

Marie hobbles back and forth, keeping a keen eye out the window for police—they want to be gone before the law shows up. The window frames her round face as she looks to the east, to the freeway and beyond. Streaking headlights cut through the rain as morning traffic scrambles down the interstate. The frumpy old building with a tiny woman peering out of it is so close to the downtown workers in suits and dresses driving in their heated cars, but Marie is so very far from them. Marie watches as a diffuse light comes to the sky, silhouetting the thirty-four-ounce ball of pure gold crowning the dome of the capitol building of California: the richest and most populous state in the United States of America: one of the richest nations on this planet.

Time to go.

Like moles, they wriggle through a hole in the wall. Marie is passed through the jagged opening by one of the big men, into the arms of another, who sets her bony body gingerly on the ground. They stand in the downpour, wordless. One by one, members of the clan shoulder their possessions. Some will catch freights and move on. A few will scout for another abandoned building to live in. Teddy and Marie watch them walk off.

Rain soaks Marie's heavy coat, glistens off Teddy's face. Teddy coughs. Marie places her arm around him. Times will get better, she whispers in his ear. Praise the Lord, she says, they just got to.

Marie hurries about, just before eviction.

Teddy and Marie outside the building.

Fred, a laid-off forklift operator from Chicago, rode the rails to California's Central Valley. He cannot find work. He sits next to the tracks in Fresno. When asked where he might be in the coming months, he buries his head in his arms and mumbles, "I might be right here."

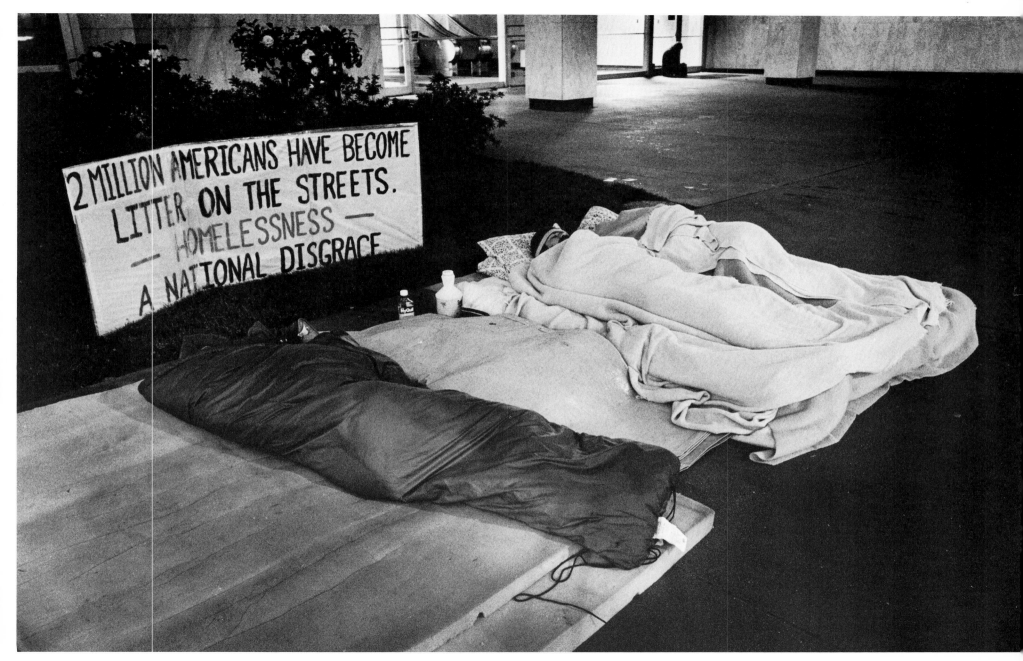

Protesters sleeping in front of a federal building, Sacramento, opposing the plight of the homeless.

GLOSSARY: Road Language Found in This Book

Newcomers to the street world will discover there is a sublanguage. Some of this vernacular dates back to the Great Depression and to before the turn of the century. Other words or expressions come straight from the economic crisis of the 1980s. To infiltrate this world properly, it helps to know its slang.

Black—A pejorative nickname some Texans have given Michigan residents, because their license plates were once this color. Many Texans hate blacks because so many have moved to the Lone Star State to compete with them for jobs.

Bull—A gun-toting railroad policeman. His job is to protect railroad cargo and keep hoboes from riding trains.

Catch-out—To leave a town on a freight train.

Crummy—Slang for caboose.

Earbang—Many rescue missions that serve free food and lodge the poor take advantage of their captive audience by requiring patrons to sit through religious services. You must be earbanged before you can eat or sleep, an experience that can last up to two hours.

Grainer—A sealed railcar that carries grain. Narrow ledges on the back of these cars are popular riding places when no boxcars are available.

Highball—A fast train.

Homeguard—A derisive term for bums or winos who do not wish to work. They hang around one town and normally don't travel. They are looked down upon by job-hunting hoboes and hitchhikers.

Hotshot—A priority train that does not stop between major cities. Hotshots are rides favored by hoboes in a hurry.

Hot yard—Rail yards are "hot" when the bull is strict about enforcing trespassing laws. Some bulls in hot yards jail rail riders. In one recent year, the Association of American

Railroads reported, bulls arrested almost sixty thousand people. In addition, bulls told the association they questioned over a half million other hoboes whom they did not arrest. Only the most clever hoboes can catch a ride out of a truly hot yard.

Jungle—Hobo camps, often filthy, vile places littered with debris, situated near rail yards. Hoboes prefer "jungling up" in woods or under bridges, but abandoned buildings, dead boxcars, and rooftops are also used.

Knuckle—The coupling that holds railroad cars together.

Mission—Houses offering free food and lodging. Missions are often run by obscure religious groups, or by organizations such as the Salvation Army. Winos once were the primary clientele. Now, some of the new poor are forced to them, though many shun missions.

New-timer—The new breed of street person, forced to the bottom by economic hardship.

On the fly—Hopping on board a moving train, an extremely dangerous practice. Veteran trainmen and hoboes alike lose their legs when they get sucked under the wheels, called "giant salami slicers" by one old-time hobo. Experienced hoboes prefer boarding trains only after they have stopped in rail yards.

Pig—A flatbed railcar that carries semitrailers piggyback, a windy but common riding place.

Rubbertramp—People who tramp about in automobiles. Rubbertramps are the elite of the road people, because they still have enough money to run their cars. In the hierarchy of the streets, they are above the hoboes and hitchhikers.

Rust Bowl—What the crippled industrial heartland is called in some circles, a modern-day equivalent of the Dust Bowl.

Sally—Short for Salvation Army.

Stamps—Government-issued food stamps.

Streamliner—Road people, especially hoboes, learn to beware of streamliners. They travel from city to city carrying no gear, only the clothes on their backs. They can be mental patients, men on the run from the law, or just really down-and-out guys. When they get cold or hungry or desperate, they can be very dangerous.

Thousand-mile blanket—Sunday newspapers, used as sheets by hoboes, big enough to last 1,000 miles. Smaller, weekday papers are hundred-mile blankets.

Units—Locomotives.